CW00951919

THE NEEDLES EXCELLENCY:

English Raised Embroidery

THE NEEDLES EXCELLENCY:

English Raised Embroidery

Edited by Lynn Hulse

London: OE Publications, 2018
ISBN 978-0-9934377-1-7

The Needles Excellency: English Raised Embroidery
Edited by Lynn Hulse

Published by OE Publications 2018
Design and production: Lamport Gilbert Ltd
Printed by Lamport Gilbert Ltd, Longmead, Shaftesbury, Dorset SP7 8PX

Set in Ideal Sans 9.5pt

Front cover: Front panel of casket, work in progress, designed by Nicola Jarvis and stitched by Karen Goldie-Morrison, detail. © Photo David Gowers.

Frontispiece: Nicola Jarvis, Design proposal for Karen Goldie-Morrison's front and back casket panels, 2014. © Nicola Jarvis.

Back cover: Casket panel 'River Yare', work in progress, designed by Nicola Jarvis and stitched by Suzanne Morton. © Photo Lynn Hulse.

Copyright remains with all contributors
ISBN: 978-0-9934377-1-7

Picture Credits

Historical introduction

Ashmolean Museum, Oxford: 1.1a-b, 1.2a–1.6, 2.3, 4.1a, 4.2a–4.9, 5.13b; Bonhams: 2.7; Elizabeth Mason and RJL Smith & Associates: 5.13a; Jacqui Carey: 3.1–3.10; David Gowers: 4.1b; Lynn Hulse: 2.8; Nicola Jarvis: 5.1–5.3a, 5.6, 5.9–5.12, 5.13c-d; Mary Evans Picture Library: 2.10; Metropolitan Museum of Art: 2.2, 2.6, 5.3b, 5.5; Sonia O'Connor: 1.1c; National Trust: 2.9a-b; Trustees of the British Museum: 5.7; Victoria and Albert Museum 2.1, 2.3, 2.4–2.5, 5.4, 5.8, 5.13a, c-d.

Catalogue

Sandra Deacon: 9.1-9.3; Sue Fowler: 10.1–10.3; David Gower: 1.1-1.2, 2.1–2.2, 3.1, 4.1–4.2, 5.1–5.3, 6.1-6.2, 7.1–7.3, 8.1, 11.1–11.3, 12.1, 12.3, 13.1, 14.1, 14.3, 15.1, 16.1, 17.1, 18.1-18.3; Lynn Hulse: 2.3, 3.2, 8.2, 8.4, 9.4, 11.4, 12.2, 13.2–13.3, 14.2, 16.2-16.3, 17.2-17.3; Nicola Jarvis: 1.3, 8.3; Jane McConnachie: 15.2.

Dedicated to the memory of our dear friend Gill Brunning
for her companionship and encouragement through
many happy hours stitching together.

Contents

Preface   8

Part A. Historical introduction

1.   Curiosities from female hands   10
   Mary M. Brooks

2.   'Surely no odder kind of needlework was ever   25
   evolved': the revival of English raised work,
   c. 1870–1930
   Lynn Hulse

3.   The language of stitch   41
   Jacqui Carey

4.   Degradation and preservation: the consequences   48
   of age and use in seventeenth-century English
   embroideries from the collection of the
   Ashmolean Museum, Oxford
   Susan M. Stanton

5.   The pencil's excellency: designing a contemporary   58
   casket in the seventeenth-century style
   Nicola Jarvis

Part B. Catalogue of contemporary raised embroidery

1.   Nicola Jarvis   72
2.   Jane Bawn   74
3.   Susanna Blackshaw   76
4.   Gill Brunning   78
5.   Kate Busby   80
6.   Aileen Cahill   82
7.   Marilyn Chalke   84
8.   Dorie Clark   86
9.   Sandra Deacon   88
10. Sue Fowler   90
11. Sally Giffen   92
12. Karen Goldie-Morrison   94
13. Deborah Jarman   96
14. Clare Lobb   98
15. Jane McConnachie   100
16. Suzanne Morton   102
17. Jenny Plumb   104
18. Ann Stainton   106

Contributors   108

Preface
Lynn Hulse

In Spring 2017, the Ashmolean Museum in Oxford hosted a six-week exhibition (25 April – 4 June) of contemporary raised work, stitched by students of *Ornamental Embroidery* under the direction of its founders, textile historian Lynn Hulse and designer-embroiderer Nicola Jarvis. *The Needles Excellency* comprised raised work caskets and picture panels inspired by the Museum's holdings of seventeenth-century English domestic needlework, including objects from the internationally renowned Mallett and Feller collections. Over four years in the making, the project was part of a continuing series of two-day workshops in the history of hand embroidery and design exploring the Ashmolean's rich collection of European and Asian decorative arts, run by *Ornamental Embroidery* through the Education Department.

The design for the casket lid, which united many of the boxes on display, was adapted from the 1673 panel *The Sacrifice of Isaac*, bequeathed to the Museum in 1947. The individual floral motifs dominating the four corners of this panel – rose, marigold, tulip and iris – were retained, but the Biblical story in the central cartouche was replaced with an oak tree and the ground covered with insects and a snail copied from seventeenth-century pattern books.

Working in a similar fashion to the pattern drawers of the past, Nicola Jarvis created a set of contemporary, bespoke designs to decorate the frieze and side panels of each casket. Seventeenth-century raised work traditionally depicts Old Testament scenes; Classical mythology; the personification of the continents, seasons and senses; architectural landmarks; flora and fauna; and, mythical creatures. The project became an heirloom piece for the students, so it seemed appropriate that the imagery on the remaining panels should have some symbolic significance while at the same time retain the spirit of the exemplars that had inspired them. Designs ranged from traditional heraldic beasts to family pets; flowers and insects; personal dwellings; motifs representing close family members both past and present; and, leisure pursuits, such as gardening and needlework.

Stitched on a ground of Duchess silk satin, the casket panels were worked in a variety of silk and metal threads combined with novelty items (glass and wooden beads, spangles, seed pearls, shells and mica), using a number of raised work techniques, including needle lace, padded, couched and wire work, combined with a range of surface stitches. The finished panels were mounted on wooden boxes specially crafted by the cabinetmaker Paul Evett.

To celebrate the opening of *The Needles Excellency*, the Education Department ran a one-day symposium exploring the Museum's collection of Stuart raised embroidery and the revival of interest in this three-dimensional technique. The topics discussed included: the cultural and economic context that fostered the development of this 'curious' work in the mid seventeenth century and its place in the education of women in English society; the disdain with which late nineteenth- and early twentieth-century scholars and practitioners expressed their opinion of raised work, and the impact this had on its renascence among embroiderers of the same period; the importance of understanding the physical language of stitch in order to "read" historic needlework; the factors that have caused seventeenth-century raised embroidery to degrade and the lessons that can be learned when it comes to preserving modern examples of the technique; and finally, designing a contemporary raised work casket in the Stuart style and the parallels between the ancient and modern practice of pattern drawing. All of the papers from the symposium are published here together with an illustrated catalogue of the caskets and picture panels displayed at the Ashmolean and in the specially curated textile galleries at the Knitting and Stitching Show 2018.

Ornamental Embroidery would like to thank Elizabeth and Micheál Feller for their generosity in granting access to their needlework collection, and, at the Ashmolean Museum, David Gowers for photography, Jude Barrett (Education Officer Adults) for the enthusiasm invested in this project and the curatorial and conservation staff for sharing their expertise, which undoubtedly enriched the students' work.

For more information about *Ornamental Embroidery and Nicola Jarvis Studio*, visit www.ornamentalembroidery.com and www.nicolajarvisstudio.co.uk

1 Curiosities from female hands
Mary M. Brooks

Introduction

Seventeenth-century raised work embroideries are fascinating and beautiful things in their own right, but they also raise many unanswered questions about the circumstances in which they were made. How do they relate to the context of their times? What did their makers think of needlework? Where were they stitching? This paper will explore the embroideries' complex and luxurious materiality, comparing them with cabinets of curiosity, and consider how their materials link to trade and empire. Their significance as a means of fashioning the virtuous woman through her 'work' will be reviewed along with the social context of their making. This paper will argue that the making is as important as the resulting made artefact. The embroideries' disappearance and survival is the final 'curiosity' to be considered.

The seventeenth century

The seventeenth century was one of the most difficult periods in English history. It witnessed regicide sanctioned by Parliament, the turmoil of the Civil Wars and the radical political experiment of the Commonwealth and the Protectorate. The re-established monarchy was constantly undermined by the lack of suitable male heirs. There were continuing tensions between Anglicanism, Roman Catholicism and the burgeoning non-conformist sects, added to which the country was beset by plague and, in the case of London, fire. Underlying all this confusion were growing urbanisation, a rising elite of city merchants, developing international trade linked to early colonisation and an on-going conversation about the place and education of women, all of which contributed to a changing sense of national identity. This seems an odd background for embroideries depicting miniature worlds filled with elaborate, highly compressed Biblical and Classical narratives set in idyllic pastoral scenes. The real and fantastical flowers and animals, fashionable rocky pools and quiet country houses with smoke rising from their multiple chimneys might be seen as a respite from the challenging realities of everyday life. Despite some common elements with contemporaneous Dutch embroideries and a legacy in colonial American needlework, these intriguingly exuberant, highly decorative works form a uniquely English tradition.[1]

Significantly, sewing was described as 'working' or 'work', a term that encompassed both plain needlework – the functional sewing learnt by those who might have to earn their living through their needle – and this fanciful, decorative embroidery, often called 'curious work' by contemporaries. The sheer number of surviving examples attests to a conspicuous consumption of leisure combined with luxurious and expensive materials in the production of such 'work' by both girls and women. This is ample evidence of a very specific feminised material culture, which had an important role in creating and making evident appropriate gendered behaviour.[2] Many raised work embroideries survive as flat panels although some were made into cushions while others were mounted professionally on boxes or made into frames for expensive mirrors. Their designs often draw on English and Continental print traditions, sometimes transferred from print to textile by professionals known as pattern drawers,[3] but the resulting embroideries fall outside the formal art historical canons. These works challenge our thinking by forcing us to question assumptions about the contexts in which they were made, their role in women's lives and their survival routes.

Making and materials

Unpicking the evidence embedded within one specific embroidery provides a useful introduction to such works and the manner of their making. *The Sacrifice of Isaac*, which inspired many of the modern caskets included in this volume, is dated and once bore the maker's initials worked in pearls. Although the letter following the initial 'I' is now missing, indents in the padded embroidery suggest this could have been 'E' or 'Y' (Fig. 1.1a). The embroidery focuses on the dramatic moment in Abraham's life when he offered up his son Isaac as a sacrifice to demonstrate his obedience to God (Genesis 22: 1-14). For young girls embroidering the story, the moral may have been the virtues of obedience to parental authority and faith in divine love. The dramatic scene of the sacrifice is highly three-dimensional with the figures constructed from applied and padded sections of detached needle lace. Isaac's head is almost completely freestanding, padded silk satin. Abraham's raised and threatening sword hand is carved wood, probably once covered with a woven fabric. His cloak is wired, making it flow as if blown by an imaginary wind. This intense encounter between the devout father and his dutiful son is enclosed in an elaborate raised cartouche, surrounded by flat and raised work birds and flowers, accompanied by a pond decorated with coral-encrusted rocks below and a cluster of elaborate buildings above.

Fig. 1.1a
Picture panel,
The Sacrifice of Isaac, 1673,
Ashmolean Museum WA OA.414. Image © Ashmolean Museum, University of Oxford.

Radiography provides new insights into the construction techniques used by the maker and the type and level of skills involved.[4] The underlying bundle of threads beneath the padded roll of detached needle lace in the cartouche becomes visible. The pearls making up the final number of the date are missing, but the direction of the drilling holes is visible in the radiograph, confirming the year as '1673'. The radiograph also reveals how Abraham's sword hand extends down the length of his sleeve. His right hand, previously invisible and unsuspected, passes behind Isaac's

Fig. 1.1b
Detail, bird's head, *The Sacrifice of Isaac*, 1673, Ashmolean Museum WA OA.414. Image © Ashmolean Museum, University of Oxford.

Fig. 1.1c
Detail, radiograph, bird's head, *The Sacrifice of Isaac*, 1673, Ashmolean Museum WA OA.414. © Sonia O'Connor.

head. Most strikingly, surprising elements of the sculptural birds were exposed. The padding and wiring of the detached needle lace wings, applied over long and short stitch "shadows", were to be expected as were the wires attaching the wooden moulds for the pears, but the glass bead forming an eye on the concealed side of the right-hand bird was unexpected. The greatest surprise was the birds' beaks (Fig. 1.1b). The radiograph shows these to be real, possibly from finches or linnets (Fig. 1.1c). Their presence raises many questions. Are they typical or atypical? Where were they obtained and prepared for use in embroideries? Could the beaks have come from singing birds which were once domestic pets belonging to the maker? Songbirds were popular additions to the fashionable household. Samuel Pepys, for example, acquired two canaries while Joseph Blagrave, writing in 1675, observed, 'The *Linnet* is a very apt Bird for any Tune or Song, if taken out of the Nest very young'.[5] Alternatively, could these beaks be the by-product of seventeenth-century cuisine? Small songbirds were certainly eaten. An instructional volume, sometimes attributed to Lady Mary Cressy, contains advice on 'the divine and moral virtues of piety, meekness, modesty, chastity, humility, compassion, temperance and affability' alongside 'cookery, preserving, candying [and] beautifying'. The author gives a recipe for baking woodcock, larks, blackbirds or sparrows with herbs, butter and egg yolks as well as instructions on the best way

Fig. 1.2a
Picture panel, *The Proclamation of Solomon*, mid to late seventeenth century, Ashmolean Museum WA 1947.191.313. Image © Ashmolean Museum, University of Oxford.

to carve pigeons and 'smaller Birds, as Larks, Sparrows, Finches, Wood-peckers, &c.'.[6] Wherever these beaks came from and whoever prepared them, they provide physical evidence for the integration of the natural and the artificial in these 'curious' works.

Surface texture and colour were clearly key in these embroideries, and were achieved by using both luxury materials and different stitches. Smooth areas worked in lustrous silk threads on a satin ground fabric would have shimmered. Silver-gilt and silver metal threads and spangles added glittering, reflective surfaces. These visual effects were enhanced by pearls and semi-precious stones such as corals, garnets and cornelians. Other natural materials were also used. A few remaining bundles of hair, yet to be identified as either human or horse hair, overlie the metal threads used to construct the maid's and King Solomon's hair in the flat panel *The Proclamation of Solomon* (1 Kings 8:54-61; see Fig. 1.2a & b).[7] Iridescent feathers twisted into threads were also used, although sadly these are often fragmentary after centuries of exposure to light and insect pests.

Fig. 1.2b
Detail of the bundles of hair overlying metal threads constructing the maid's hair in *The Proclamation of Solomon,* mid to late seventeenth century, Ashmolean Museum WA 1947.191.313. Image © Ashmolean Museum, University of Oxford.

Trading the world's bounty

While the beads, coral and semi-precious stones link these pieces to the natural world – a source of wonder and scientific study – they also demonstrate international trade patterns and with this, exploitative attitudes to the nations and natural resources of the world. Coral, with all its religious and mythological significance, was extracted from the Mediterranean and traded, often through Antwerp, from Europe to India.[8] Although native freshwater pearls were available, particularly from Scotland, complex trading routes brought pearls on the reverse journey from India and the Persian Gulf to England. Following the lead of Spanish colonisers in the Americas, the East India Company (EIC), chartered in 1600, was quickly involved in this lucrative trade.[9] In India, the EIC battled with the Dutch East India Company (*Verenigde Oost-Indische Compagnie,* founded in 1602) for the trade in garnets, spinels and other semi-precious stones.[10] Alongside such luxury goods, quantities of decorative feathers were imported into Europe for ornamenting hats, fans and interiors.[11] London port books record the arrival of £1,863's worth of feathers in 1559/60.[12] The Court Minutes of the EIC for 3 February 1618 include a note for a 'Bargain to be concluded for certain frames, feathers, and pictures'.[13] The Company

Fig. 1.3
The Four Continents, mid to late seventeenth century, Feller collection, Ashmolean Museum WA 2014.71.55. Image © Ashmolean Museum, University of Oxford.

permitted private trade amongst its officers independent of its own trading activities. Such "permission" goods encompassed ostrich feathers.[14]

Local and global worlds co-exist in the embroidery *The Four Continents* (Fig. 1.3).[15] The central oval panel shows an idealised scene of ploughing, harvesting, fishing and tending sheep. This rural world is surrounded by personifications of the four continents, probably based on prints by Wither, published first by William Marshall and then re-issued by Peter Stent.[16] The use of distinct embroidery techniques – tent stitch for the countryside and raised work for the exotic figures – highlights their differences. America is a seated man, wearing a feathery headdress and skirt, holding a bow and arrow. It is tempting to imagine that this outfit might bear some resemblance to the feathered clothing Aphra Behn describes in her semi-autobiographical 1688 novel *Oroonoko*: 'little short habits' with 'glorious wreaths for their heads, necks, arms and legs, whose tinctures are unconceivable'.[17] Africa is represented by a man holding a leafy branch, possibly sweet balsam. Both Asia and Europe are women, the former holding a censor and seated next to a camel, the latter a crowned queen clutching a book, possibly the Bible.[18]

With this evocation of wider mercantile and political horizons come more complex issues. An embroidered mirror frame depicting female personifications of Hearing, Touch and Smell includes a stylish courtier greeting Smell by doffing his hat (Fig. 1.4a).[19] The embroiderer has only worked the lavish feather plume although the shaded underdrawing shows the hat clearly (Fig. 1.4b). This is probably the type of beaver hat so brilliantly discussed by Timothy Brook in *Vermeer's Hat*. Mapping the links between the trade in beaver fur and the soldier in Vermeer's painting *Officer and Laughing Girl* (1685), Brook highlights the connections between fashion, exploration and exploitation in the New World.[20] The North American beaver was almost rendered extinct by European demand for its fur. The feather, too, evokes not just the dashing glamour of cavalier style but also the depredation of the natural world, supported by exploitative social, political and trading systems. A grimmer world of reality lies beyond these "charming" figures.

Cabinets of curiosity

This material world could also be used as a way of thinking, physically expressed in the formation of cabinets of curiosity *(Kunstkammer)*, which brought together the natural *(naturalia)* and the made *(artificialia)*. Created from the sixteenth century onwards, such cabinets demonstrated both the intellectual curiosity and the connoisseurship of the collectors. 'The Ark', the collection formed by John Tradescant (c. 1570–1638) and his son John (1608–1662), is probably the most famous English cabinet of curiosity. Open to visitors from the 1630s, it included 'Divers various and beautifully coloured feathers of Birds from the West India's' as well as 'cloth spun of the downe of yellow feathers'.[21] Alongside the usual mermaid

Fig. 1.4a
*Mirror frame,
Ladies
personifying the
Sense of
Hearing, Touch
and Smell,*
second half of
the
seventeenth
century, Feller
collection,
Ashmolean
Museum WA
2014.71.6. Image
© Ashmolean
Museum,
University of
Oxford.

(in this instance, only a hand) and a cup made from a unicorn's horn, the cabinet displayed white, black and red branched and unbranched coral as well as 'severall things rarely cut in coral'.[22] Peter Mundy's 1634 description of the Tradescants' collection of curiosities as comprising 'beasts, fowle, fishes, serpents, wormes... pretious stones... a little garden with divers outlandish herbes and flowers' also evokes the crowded landscapes of English raised work.[23] This is not to imply that any contemporary would have considered such embroideries to be the equivalent of the cabinets of curiosity but they do exhibit some of the same wide-ranging interests, albeit in a much less systematic or encyclopaedic way. As the beaks, hair and feathers demonstrate, nature is physically part of these pieces along with the repeated depiction of natural and mythical creatures, as well as familiar and exotic flowers. The coral and gemstones collected for cabinets of curiosity are integrated into these embroideries, and as such, they are striking examples of *artificialia* incorporating *naturalia*.[24]

Learning to 'work'

Affluent schoolgirls and women working at home clearly dedicated – or were made to dedicate – considerable time and energy, not to mention money, to their production. Many of these pieces were made as 'curious' fancy embroidery rather than plain needlework, and formed a key element in the training of well-off girls from elite and aspiring families, whether educated at home or in one of the many thriving boarding schools. The argument for this work being made in the schoolroom has been discussed elsewhere.[25] The note associated with the Ashmolean Museum's pre-1665 box is a rare statement linking the maker and her school: 'The cabinet was made by my Mother's Grandmother who was educated at Hackney School' (Fig. 1.5a & b).[26] Mrs Playford's school in Islington offered a typical curriculum of 'all manner of Curious Works, as also Reading, Writing, Music, Dancing and the French Language'.[27] It is surely not accidental that embroidery heads the list. Reformers such as Mary Astell (1666–1731) attempted to develop the curriculum for girls to include more serious subjects, but needlework remained central, and was thought critical in developing and demonstrating feminine

Fig. 1.4b
Courtier greeting 'Smell' by doffing his hat, Mirror frame, *Ladies personifying the Sense of Hearing, Touch and Smell,* second half of the seventeenth century, Feller collection, Ashmolean Museum WA 2014.71.6. Image © Ashmolean Museum, University of Oxford.

Fig. 1.5a
Box, *Scenes from the Life of Abraham,* before 1665, Ashmolean Museum WA 1947.191.315. Image © Ashmolean Museum, University of Oxford.

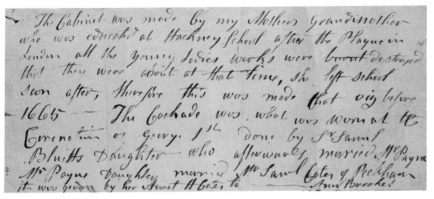

The Cabinet was made by my Mothers Grandmother who was educated at Hackney school after the Plague in London all the young ladies works were burnt destroyed that they wear about at that time, she left school soon after, therefore this was made that very before 1665 — The Cockade was what was worn at the Coronation of Geory. 1st done by Sr James Blunts Daughter who afterwards married Mrs Payne Mr Poyns Daughter married Mr Saml Coter of Peckham it was given by her Aunt A Cotes to Ann Brookes

Fig. 1.5b
Note accompanying the box, *Scenes from the Life of Abraham*, before 1665, Ashmolean Museum WA 1947.191.315. Image © Ashmolean Museum, University of Oxford.

qualities.[28] Margaret Cavendish, Duchess of Newcastle (1623–1673) was not afraid to express her concern over girls' education: 'The breeding [i.e. education] of men were after a different manner of ways from those of women'.[29]

The contradictory quality of homogeneity and variance in these embroideries may be a result of their manner of making and, of course, the identity of the individual who chose both the narrative and the images is rarely known. The homogeneity derives from the use of printed sources for figures, flora and fauna. Motifs are endlessly repeated but in different combinations. Presumably, the embroiderer – or her teacher or mother – could go to the pattern drawer and ask for a central story, then select the buildings, ponds, animals and flowers to accompany it. Variation comes from the combination of motifs and their stitched interpretation. This is where contemporaries perceived originality and individuality to lie. Hannah Woolley, the Martha Stewart of her day, wrote books on teaching aspirational gentlewomen fashionable domestic skills. She offered lessons on embroidery, stressing the importance of imagination and innovation in stitching:

> ... and many fancies which were after my own fancy, not at all to imitate others; for there is nothing which I hate more, than to work as a Child doth after a Sampler: That brain that can invent nothing, is good for nothing; nor there is nothing which I more love than Invention...[30]

'...my chief help'

Few women wrote about their feelings towards their needlework; perhaps the numerous unfinished embroideries are the best witnesses here. However, these are still indicators of time spent and virtue to be gained in the act of stitching itself. Others resisted. In *The Womens Sharpe Revenge* (1639), the pseudonymous 'Mary Tattle-well' and 'Joan Hit-Him-Home' argue that women were denied education and forced to do needlework to keep them subordinate: '... we are set onely to the Needle to pricke our fingers'.[31] The rare examples, fictional and factual, of women reflecting on what they felt about their embroidery have been discussed elsewhere but it is useful to review the limited evidence here.[32] Artesia in Emanuel Ford's 1607 romance *Ornatus and Artesia* finds delight and diversion in hers when under emotional stress, a sentiment shared by Lady Anne Clifford (1590–1676) who felt her 'work' was her 'chief help to pass away the time' during an unhappy marriage.[33] Both she and Lady Margaret Hoby (1571–1633) record doing their needlework alone and with companions, sometimes while listening to sacred or secular literature. Lady Margaret wrote in her diary: 'After prairs, I wrought, as I was accustomed, with my maides, and hard Mr Ardington read' (12 August 1601).[34] This activity seems to have taken place in a shared public space in the house as Lady Margaret specifically describes her companions joining her in her chamber when she was unwell: '... kept my chamber, and, as I was able, I wrought and reede and had Mr Ardington to read to me' (26 March 1601).[35] The Puritan Elizabeth Walker (1623–1690) felt guilty about the pleasure she found in her needlework, a diversion from her household duties and spiritual contemplation: 'She was Mistress of her needle to that degree, that she would blame herself that she had spent so much time and industry, to attain it in worsted, silk and finest Thread'.[36]

Creating gender, social status and moral worth

Embroidery helped to create the seventeenth-century goodly and godly woman. It was an act which developed self-control within a culturally acceptable framework and avoided the dangerous traps that lay in wait for young readers. It established patterns of appropriate conduct with a social gloss which codified a suitable status and a background of appropriate financial resources – the fathers and brothers who paid for the schooling and materials. This investment would hopefully enable girls to gain a husband and thus social and financial security. The physically controlled body required by stitching should be paralleled by an equally controlled mind, reflecting on higher things. Moralists are keen to stress that pleasure in needlework ought to be avoided least the sin of idleness be replaced by that of pride. John Taylor constantly sought to reinforce its high status, arguing 'The noble worth of Needle-workes high grace' was associated with 'mighty Queenes' and 'high borne Ladies'.[37] 'Work' made the girl – and it was the making that counted. Enabling the 'worker' to demonstrate not only her skills but also her moral probity and socially acceptable feminine conformity seems to have been as important as the expensive materials, the cost of commissioning the design and of learning the requisite technical skills.

Disappearance and survival

'Curious work' abruptly became unfashionable in England early in the eighteenth century. Embroiderers continued to draw on the same Biblical themes but the robust three-dimensional style became etiolated. Seventeenth-century

Fig. 1.6
Picture panel, *Jephthah and his Daughter*, mid to late seventeenth century, Feller collection, Ashmolean Museum WA 2014.71.57. Image © Ashmolean Museum, University of Oxford.

embroideries, once cherished, seem to have gone underground. The little available evidence suggests they survived almost unseen by passing through the female line, thus paralleling the practice of learning needlework as a female tradition, transmitted from mothers to daughters or teachers to schoolgirls. Jane Harrison, wife of Edmund, Embroiderer to Charles I and Charles II, willed 'the satin stitched picture that was her sisters worke' to her elder daughter.[38] A descendant of the schoolgirl who made the Ashmolean box records it 'was made by my Mother's Grandmother' and was 'given by her Aunt H Cotes – to Ann Brookes' (Fig. 1.5b).[39] Some pieces were evidently cherished by eighteenth-century embroiderers, who integrated them into their own work. For example, one seventeenth-century beadwork depiction of the tragic story of Jephthah's daughter (Judges 11) has an eighteenth-century embroidered frame (Fig. 1.6).[40] The complicated process of re-evaluating the aesthetic and cultural value of these works only began in the late nineteenth and early twentieth centuries.[41]

Conclusion

The meaning and values which contemporaries attached to 'curious' works was clearly complex and influenced their survival and their almost perverse invisibility in later centuries. The complexity of these objects and the sometimes startling evidence they contain should not divert us from re-evaluating not only the made object but also the value accrued from the process of making.

Acknowledgements

My thanks go to Elizabeth and Micheál Feller for their extraordinary generosity in sharing their collection; for photography, Richard Holdsworth; Dr Sonia O'Connor, previously of the University of Bradford, and Mark Norman, previously of the Ashmolean Museum, for radiography; Professor Catherine Whistler, Keeper of Western Art, Ashmolean Museum; and, Dr Lynn Hulse, *Ornamental Embroidery*.

Notes

[1] For example, a late seventeenth-century Flemish ebony cabinet with raised work embroidery panels sold at Christies' in 2002, https://www.christies.com/lotfinder/Lot/a-flemish-ebony-and-embroidered-raised-work-table-4001997-details.aspx

[2] Such 'work' was seen as an emasculating activity in the domestic context. In Chapman's 1602 eponymous play, Sir Giles Goosecappe is mocked for his ability at plain and fancy needlework: 'Hee is the best Sempster of any woman in England, and will worke you needle worke edgings, and French purles from an Angell to foure Angells a yearde... He will make you flyes and wormes of all sortes most liuely, and is now working a whole bed embroidred with nothing but glowe wormes'; George Chapman, *Sir Gyles Goosecappe* (London: John Windet, 1606), Act 2, Scene 1. Professional embroiderers were usually men, although women were also involved.

[3] John Nevinson, 'John Nelham embroiderer', *Bulletin of the Needle & Bobbin Club,* vol. 65, nos 1-2 (1982), pp. 17-19; Margaret Swain, 'John Nelham's needlework panel', *Bulletin of the Needle & Bobbin Club,* vol. 65, nos 1-2 (1982), pp. 3-16.

[4] For a further discussion of the radiography of this piece, see Mary M. Brooks and Sonia O'Connor, '"In needle works there doth great knowledge rest": The contribution of X-radiography to the understanding of seventeenth-century English embroideries from the Ashmolean Museum of Art and Archaeology, Oxford', in *X-radiography of Textiles, Dress and Related Objects,* edited by Sonia A. O'Connor and Mary M. Brooks (Oxford: Elsevier, 2007), pp. 237-248 at pp. 238-240.

[5] Samuel Pepys, 'This night comes two cages, which I bought this evening for my canary birds', *Diary,* 25 January 1661, D. S. Grey, Samuel Pepys online, 2002–2018, available at: http://www.pepys.info/1661/1661jan.html [accessed 4 March 2018]. Joseph Blagrave, *New Additions to the Art of Husbandry ... with Directions for Breeding and Ordering all sorts of Singing-birds* (London: Benjamin Billingsley, 1675), p. 118.

[6] Anon ('A Lady'), *The Whole Duty of a Woman,* 2nd edn (London: J. Gwillim, 1696), p. 128.

[7] See Mary M. Brooks, *English Embroideries of the Sixteenth and Seventeenth Centuries in the Collection of the Ashmolean Museum* (Oxford & London: Ashmolean Museum/ Jonathan Horne Publications, 2004), pp. 48-49.

[8] Marlise Rijks, '"Unusual Excrescences of Nature": Collected coral and the study of petrified luxury in early modern Antwerp', *Dutch Crossing,* vol. 4 (2017), pp. 1-29.

[9] R. A. Donkin, *Beyond Price: Pearls and Pearl-fishing: Origins to the Age of Discoveries* (Philadelphia: American Philosophical Society, 1998), p. 168.

[10] David W. Davies, *A Primer of Dutch Seventeenth Century Overseas Trade* ([Hague]: Springer Science & Business Media, 2013 [1961]), p. 84.

[11] From the sixteenth century onwards, trade networks, often with links to Jewish diaspora communities, were importing such exotic commodities into Western Europe; Jonathan I. Israel, *Diasporas Within a Diaspora: Jews, Crypto-Jews and the World of Maritime Empires 1540-1740* (Leiden: Brill, 2002), p. 5.

[12] It is not clear whether these feathers were for decorative or functional uses, such as feather beds, but the list for 1565/66 contains several new commodities given without valuation. These include 'flowers of feathers', which presumably were decorative; see *The particular valew of certayne necessary and vnnecessarye wares brought into the Porte of London in the second year of the Quenes Majestis reigne, the ouerquantyte wherof lamentably spoylith the realme yearly* (S.P. 12/8, ff. 63-69) and *Wares brought in to London* (Michaelmas 1565; Lans. 8, ff. 75-76) cited in Brian Dietz, ed., 'Appendix III: Value of imports,

1559/60 and 1565/66' in *The Port and Trade of Early Elizabethan London: Documents* (London: London Record Society, 1972), pp. 152-155, available at: British History Online http://www.british-history.ac.uk/london-record-soc/vol8/ pp 152-155 [accessed 6 March 2018].

[13] East Indies, China and Japan: February 1618 (1–15th) Court Minutes in W. Noel Sainsbury, ed., *Calendar of State Papers Colonial, East Indies, China and Japan, Volume 3, 1617–1621* (London: Her Majesty's Stationery Office, 1870), pp. 115-129, available at: *British History Online* http://www. british-history.ac.uk/cal-state-papers/colonial/east-indies-china-japan/ vol3/pp115-129 [accessed 6 March 2018].

[14] Other 'permitted' items included agate, diamonds, pearls and tortoiseshell; see Maxine Berg, Felicia Gottmann, Hanna Hodacs and Chris Nierstrasz, eds, *Goods from the East, 1600-1800: Trading Eurasia* (New York: Palgrave Macmillan, 2015), p. 158. The Company reserved the right to trade for itself in Carmenia wool, cotton yarn and silk; see *The Records of Fort St. George: Despatches from England,* vol. 48 (Madras, 1931), pp. 57-58, cited in Timothy Davies, 'British Private Trade Networks in the Arabian Seas, c. 1680– c. 1760' (PhD dissertation, Warwick University, 2012), pp. 242-243, available at: http://wrap.warwick.ac.uk/56346/1/ WRAP_THESIS_Davies_2012.pdf [accessed 2 February 2018].

[15] Mary M. Brooks, Elizabeth Feller and Jacqueline Holdsworth, *Micheál & Elizabeth Feller: The Needlework Collection,* vol. I ([Hascombe]: Needleprint, 2011), pp. 72-75.

[16] This depiction of the Continents is close to the figures on a mirror frame in the Lady Lever Collection (LL5219); see Xanthe Brooke, *Catalogue of Embroideries. The Lady Lever Art Gallery* (Stroud: Alan Sutton/National Museums & Galleries on Merseyside, 1992), pp. 193-194. The same personifications with their names noted beside them are on a beadwork piece dated 1691 in the Metropolitan Museum of Art (59.208.68); see Andrew Morrall and Melinda Watt, eds, *English Embroidery from the Metropolitan Museum of Art, 1580–1700. 'Twixt Art and Nature* (New Haven/London: Yale University Press, Bard Graduate Center & Metropolitan Museum of Art, 2008), pp. 288-289.

[17] Behn presented 'the dress of the Indian Queen', which she brought back from her extraordinary journey to Surinam (then the British West Indies), to the King's Theatre, London, for use as theatrical costume; Aphra Behn, *Oroonoko, or, The Royal Slave: a True History* (London: Will. Canning, 1688), p. 5.

[18] For a discussion of these personifications and the seventeenth-century ideal woman, see Heather A. Hughes, 'The Four Continents in seventeenth-century embroidery and the making of English femininity'. in M. Melion and B. Ramakers, eds, *Personification: Embodying Meaning and Emotion* (Leiden: Brill, 2016), pp. 716-794.

[19] Brooks et al, *Feller: The Needlework Collection,* pp. 72-75.

[20] Timothy Brook, *Vermeer's Hat. The Seventeenth Century and the Dawn of the Global World* (London: Bloomsbury Press, 2009), pp. 26–46.

[21] John Tradescant, *Musaeum Tradescantianum: or, A Collection of Rarities* (London: Grismond, 1656), pp. 2 and 37.

[22] Tradescant, op. cit. pp. 36 and 52.

[23] Peter Mundy, *The Travels of Peter Mundy in Europe and Asia, 1608–1667* (London: Hakluyt Society, 1919), vol. III, p. i.

[24] For a further discussion of curiosity and seventeenth-century embroideries, see Mary M. Brooks, 'Performing curiosity: re-viewing women's domestic embroidery in seventeenth-century England', *The Seventeenth Century,* vol. 32, no. 1 (2017), pp. 1-29.

[25] See, for example, Mary M. Brooks, 'Learning the skills' in Brooks et al, *Feller: The Needlework Collection,* pp. 14-16 and Ruth Geuter, 'Embroidered Biblical narratives and their social context' in Morrall and Watt, *'Twixt Art and Nature,* pp. 57-77, at pp. 62-64.

[26] See Brooks, *English Embroideries,* pp. 10-11 and 40-43.

[27] From an advertisement in the 1659 edition of *Select Ayres and Dialogues,* published by her husband, the music collector and publisher John Playford.

[28] Mary Astell, *A Serious Proposal to the Ladies for the Advancement of their True and Greatest Interest* (London: Wilkin, 1694).

[29] Margaret Cavendish, *A True Relation of my Birth, Breeding, and Life. Published as an addendum to Natures Pictures Drawn by Fancies Pencil to the Life,* in Sylvia Bowerbank and Sara Mendelson, eds, *Paper Bodies. A Margaret Cavendish Reader* (Ontario: Broadview Literary Texts, 2000), p. 43.

[30] Hannah Wooley, *A Supplement to The Queen-like Closet, or, A Little of Everything presented to all ingenious Ladies, and Gentlewomen* (London: T. R. for Richard Lownds, 1674), p. 80.

[31] *The Womens Sharpe Revenge: or an Answer to Sir Seldome Sober* (London: O[kes], 1640), p. 41. Ironically given John Taylor's prominence as the author of *The Prayse of the Needle* (1631), this was a response to his misogynistic *Juniper Lecture* (1639).

[32] See, for example, Mary M. Brooks, 'Needlework and Reading', in Brooks et al, *Feller: The Needlework Collection,* pp. 58-59.

[33] Emanuel Ford, *The most pleasant Historie of Ornatus and Artesia* (London: Creede, 1607), Chapter 3, n. p.; David J. H. Clifford, *The Diaries of Lady Anne Clifford* (Stroud: Sutton Publishing, 1992), p. 43.

[34] Joanna Moody, ed., *The Private Life of an Elizabethan Lady. The Diary of Lady Margaret Hoby, 1599–1605* (Stroud: Sutton Publishing, 1998), p. 159.

[35] Moody, op. cit., p. 140.

[36] [Anthony Walker], *The Holy Life of Mrs Elizabeth Walker* (London: Leake, 1690), p. 67.

[37] John Taylor, 'The Praise of the Needle', in *The Needle's Excellency* (London: Boler, 1631), p. [4].

[38] Patricia Wardle, 'The King's embroiderer: Edmund Harrison', *Textile History,* vol. 25, no. 1, (1994), pp. 29-59 at p. 46.

[39] See Brooks, *English Embroideries,* pp. 40-43.

[40] Brooks et al, *Feller: The Needlework Collection,* pp. 24-25.

[41] Mary M. Brooks, '"Another freak of fashion": Collectors, collecting, connoisseurship and changing views of 17th century English embroideries', *Text,* vol. 39 (2011–12), pp. 12-17.

2 'Surely no odder kind of needlework was ever evolved': the revival of English raised work, c. 1870 – 1930
Lynn Hulse

Introduction

The revival of interest in historic textiles during the Victorian period led to a renewed appreciation for English embroidery made before 1800. One of the more obscure branches of needlecraft to be rediscovered and re-evaluated was Stuart raised work, described by the interwar art critic Frank Davis as 'an odd episode of history in a minor art'.[1] The cultural significance of this style of embroidery, popular in England during the middle decades of the seventeenth-century, was slow to materialise. The London evening newspaper *The Pall Mall Gazette* reported in 1912 that 'Some time ago this work was not much noticed, but now it is considered very curious and valuable, both on account of its age and eccentricity'.[2] Yet, as Mary Brooks has demonstrated, it was to be another twenty years before the aesthetic value of Stuart raised work was widely recognised by collectors and connoisseurs.[3] This paper illuminates the various reasons why historians and practitioners of the late nineteenth and early twentieth centuries should have so derided the technique and how that might have limited its renascence during this period.

Stuart raised work rediscovered

In March 1873, Princess Helena, President of the School of Art Needlework,[4] asked the Committee of Council on Education to host 'an Exhibition of Ancient Needlework' at the South Kensington Museum.[5] The request, which was made 'in the interests of Art Education and the employment of women',[6] was duly granted and the opening of the *Special Loan Exhibition of Decorative Art Needlework* was scheduled for later that season. An advisory committee made up of experts, collectors and artists recommended that the display should exhibit specimens of embroidery noted for their artistic, archaeological and historical merits. Several ladies associated with the School were charged with the task of inviting lenders, and advertisements were placed in the national press in the search for suitable items.[7] Over 170 British and French owners responded. The ensuing exhibition contained around 700 embroideries dating from the early Middle Ages to the end of the eighteenth century, divided into nineteen classes ranging from ecclesiastical and domestic needlework to costume and accessories.

Class IV, entitled 'Embroidery on Work-Boxes, and as Pictures, etc.', featured seventeenth-century English raised work – the first occasion on which such pieces had been widely displayed in public, though the South Kensington Museum had already begun acquiring examples of the technique a decade earlier.[8] Among the exhibits were picture panels, book covers, cushions, mirror frames and caskets, including the box illustrated in Fig. 2.1, signed 'E. C.' and dated 1678.[9]

The specimens were variously described in the exhibition catalogue as 'raised work', 'raised needlework', 'raised figures' or 'parts in relief',[10] after the nomenclature found in English seventeenth-century printed sources like John Taylor's poem 'The Praise of the Needle', published in *The Needles Excellency* (London, 1631), and 'The School Mistris Terms of Art for all her ways of Sowing' listed in Randall Holmes's encyclopaedic work *The Academy of Armory, or, A Storehouse of Armory and Blazon* (Chester, 1688).[11]

In the wake of the *Special Loan Exhibition*, Caulfeild and Saward's 1882 *Dictionary of Needlework* became the first textile publication of the nineteenth century to

Fig. 2.1
Casket embroidered by 'E. C.' (possibly Elizabeth Coombe), 1678, V&A T.43-1954. © Victoria and Albert Museum, London.

discuss Stuart raised work. Saward's historical survey of 'Embroidery' referred to a 'peculiar kind' of raised work known as 'Embroidery on the Stamp' – the earliest printed reference to this term – and outlined the salient features of the technique.[12]

Secondary sources and how-to manuals printed since the *Dictionary of Needlework* have tended to gloss over the etymology of the term 'on the stamp' or 'stump work', while those which have attempted to give a definition, occasionally refer to the wooden moulds used to create the raised elements.[13] However, John Nevinson, Assistant Keeper in the Department of Textiles (1931–1939) at the Victoria and Albert Museum (V&A), summarily dismissed this view:

> ... for about two hundred years after the technique died out, there is no trace of either "stump" or "on the stamp" in books, inventories, or documents, nor can any meaning be attached to the word or phrase, though perverted ingenuity has made the unlikely guess that the carved wooden heads for the miniature figures... were called "stumps".[14]

Due in large part to these efforts, Stuart raised work had sufficiently entered the public consciousness by the early 1890s for its qualities to be debated by commentators writing about the decorative arts. The revival of interest in the technique ran parallel to the development of art embroidery. Since the Renaissance, textiles had occupied an inferior position in Western art. William Morris and his circle sought to bridge the gulf separating the "greater" (painting, sculpture and architecture) and "lesser" arts (decorative art and handicraft) and, in so doing, elevate embroidery from a domestic craft to a serious art form, a goal widely shared by the press in its coverage of the 1873 exhibition. Highlighting the 'utter degeneracy of modern so-called "fancy" needlework', the lady's newspaper *The Queen* anticipated that 'good secular ornamental needlework, well designed after the best old models and carried out in rich and harmonious colouring with all the wealth of ancient stitchery, may once more be seen in our houses.'[15] *The Art Journal*, the leading organ of Victorian art criticism, hoped that the exhibition might 'induce ladies to practice *true* embroidery, which is essentially an Art-production, and give scope for the display of talent, instead of wasting their time in mechanically filling up German woolwork'.[16] The latter, a type of shading in cross or tent stitch from a pattern printed on squared paper, had eclipsed most other forms of embroidery by the second quarter of the nineteenth century, resulting in a general decline in needle skills. Scholars and practitioners, particularly those associated with the Arts and Crafts movement, believed that art embroidery was only achieved through the conjoining of technical skill, born of an in-depth study of old examples, with originality in the selection and arrangement of colours, the choice of suitable materials and above all, good design. It was by these criteria that the artistic and technical merits of both ancient and modern needlework would be measured.

'One man's meat is another man's poison'

The textile historian Rachel Head (1860–1936) summed up contemporary attitudes towards Stuart raised embroidery when she wrote in 1904, 'Surely no odder kind of needlework was ever evolved'.[17] Writers sympathetic to the technique often described it in somewhat patronising terms as 'quaint', 'curious', or 'eccentric',[18] while more outspoken critics found it 'tasteless', 'very ugly and barbarous', 'a debased form of needlework', and even proclaimed it 'innocent of any pretensions to art'.[19] The social historian and practitioner Therle Hughes subsequently concluded that 'No other form of English embroidery has provoked such derision among later needlewomen'.[20] In order to understand why Stuart raised work should have aroused such disdain, one must look to the value that scholars and practitioners placed on design and technical skill.[21]

'Stump work' was lambasted not only for its simplistic patterns and lack of artistic expression when compared with the work of medieval embroiderers but also for its total disregard for the principles of good design. Ignoring the laws of balance, harmony and proportion, the technique placed too much emphasis on an overabundance of disparate elements that cluttered any sense of visual unity.

In its review of the *Special Loan Exhibition*, *The Art Journal* highlighted the naivety of the designs: 'The quaint appearance of the embroidery on workboxes... might induce the uninitiated to consider it of an early period, but it is all of the sixteenth and seventeenth centuries.'[22] This sentiment was echoed in *Needlework as Art*, published in 1886 by Lady Marian Alford (1817–1888), Vice-President of the Royal School of Art Needlework (RSAN). Discussing the historic development of Stuart embroidery, Lady Alford posited:

> The drawing and design were childish, and show us how high art can in a century slip back into no art at all. Any one comparing the Dunstable or Fishmongers' pall [both masterpieces of *Opus Anglicanum*] with one of the best caskets of this period would say that the latter should have preceded the former by centuries.[23]

Disciples of the Gothic revival wrote disparagingly of the manner in which flora and fauna were executed in Stuart raised work compared with the practice found in medieval decoration. In a lecture given to The Royal Society of Arts in 1905, for example, the textile historian Alan Summerly Cole (1846–1934) drew attention to the 'grotesque' birds ornamenting one box in the V&A, which he argued, were no match for the marginal illuminations so 'vigorously expressed' in manuscripts dating some three hundred years earlier.[24] Raised work figures were equally derided. The designer and craftswoman May Morris (1862–1938) contemned the 'foolish flat pudding-faces' (Fig. 2.2) – described by one newspaper reviewer as 'painfully suggestive of a rag doll' – preferring instead the poignant expression of human emotion portrayed in English medieval embroidery.[25]

Historians and practitioners also found the compositions used in Stuart raised work amusing to the point of being ludicrous for their total failure to observe any discernable laws of scale and proportion. In the opinion of the needlewoman Ellen Masters, butterflies half the size of figures and acorns and strawberries as large as heads 'raise a smile' (Fig. 2.3).[26] May Morris found one panel depicting the Old Testament story of *Hagar and Ishmael* so 'irresistibly funny' and 'joyously absurd' that she devoted several column inches to it. Her description doesn't quite match the embroidered version acquired by the V&A in around 1878 but there are enough features in common to illustrate the point (Fig. 2.4): 'the fingers in a lamentable state of limpness, languishing in all directions like old gloves', 'the bulgy curtains' and 'an angel who leans down across a dark blue wooden fence (meant to represent a cloud, doubtless) surveying the scene with intense surprise – as well he may – with hands outspread and eyes staring.'[27]

Fig. 2.2
Mirror frame with *Jael and Barak*, 1672, detail, Metropolitan Museum of Art 39.13.2a.
© Metropolitan Museum of Art, New York.

Fig. 2.3
Mirror frame, *Ladies personifying the Senses of Hearing, Touch and Smell*, second half of the seventeenth century, detail, Feller collection Ashmolean Museum WA 2014.71.6. Image reproduced with kind permission of Ashmolean Museum, University of Oxford.

Fig. 2.4
Embroidered
picture, *Hagar
and Ishmael*,
1660–1690,
V&A 125-1878.
© Victoria and
Albert Museum,
London.

Fig. 2.5
Embroidered
picture, *Esther
and Ahaseurus*,
1660–1690,
V&A 892-1864.
© Victoria and
Albert Museum,
London.

The desire to cram as much as possible into the picture plane (Fig. 2.5) was also widely ridiculed. As the furniture and design historian Margaret Jourdain (1876–1951) observed: 'When the figures... have been arranged, the one object of the worker appears to have been to leave no inch of the background uncovered, and with this aim animals, insects, flowers, fruit-bearing trees, castles, ornamental fish-ponds, are crowded together without any congruity'.[28] This practice was completely at odds with contemporary aesthetics. The designer Selwyn Image (1849–1930) strongly advised art embroiderers to aim at simplicity, not to overfill their work with an abundance of different elements, 'which produce a sense of confusion and irritation, and in reality, prove only a poverty of invention.'[29] May Morris took this one step further, advising her students to 'make your spaces interesting, for restraint tells as much as profusion [if not] more'.[30]

In a similar vein, critics denigrated 'stump work' for its lack of thematic co-ordination, in which Biblical subjects were juxtaposed with historical personages and contemporary events,[31] and figures dressed in the prevailing fashions of the Stuart period were arranged in scenes played out in front of modern buildings. It was perhaps these contradictions and anachronisms that constituted raised work's ultimate sin in the eyes of some modern viewers. As *The Art Journal* argued, the desire for realistic fidelity – 'so fortunate for... [later] human and historical interest' – eventually led to raised embroidery's 'artistic destruction'.[32]

When it came to technical skill, practitioners vigorously debated the unnecessary intricacy of the stitches and the multiplicity of materials utilised in 'stump work'. Lady Alford was appalled by the '[i]nfinite trouble and ingenuity wasted on looking-glass frames, picture frames, and caskets', while Mary Thomas (1889–1948), an authority on embroidery technique, bemoaned the endless amount of labour expended on fine stitchery.[33] May Morris focused her invective on the 'interminably fine lace stitches' that were a common feature of the work: '... here we see a waste of energy that, seriously, is lamentable – days, weeks, even months, of human life embodied in this rag-doll nonsense for the next generation to laugh at.'[34]

Somewhat surprisingly, textile historians like the Marshalls admired the inventiveness and effort exerted on the minutest details, and believed that 'the crudeness of the designs [was] atoned for by the extreme beauty of the *technique*'.[35] Indeed, A. J. B. Wace, deputy keeper of textiles (1924–1934) at the V&A, found certain caskets to be '[e]xquisitely worked'.[36] So too Eugenie Gibson, who reckoned that the skillful endeavours of seventeenth-century workers deserved 'warm admiration'.[37] Even Rachel Head grudgingly admitted that Stuart raised work had 'a fascination of its own by reason of the marvellous skill and ingenuity by which its innumerable component parts... have been wrought more or less into a harmonious whole with the aid of a variety of fine and intricate stitches.'[38] *The Art Journal* went so far as to claim that in the finer pieces belonging to the collector Viscountess Wolseley, 'there is enough technique to furnish a whole school of embroiderers. Half-a-dozen samplers… would hardly give so great a variety of stitch.'[39] Nevertheless, the exuberant response of textile historians ran counter to the practice and values of art embroiderers, who chose to employ a small vocabulary of stitches, in the belief that 'excellence of workmanship does not lie in many curious and difficult varieties of stitch, but in the expressive use of a few ordinary ones.'[40]

The raised elements characteristic of 'stump work' also caused a stir in some quarters. In his 1905 publication *English Embroidery*, A. F. Kendrick, Keeper of Textiles (1897–1924) at the V&A, described the excessive padding as 'a mockery of sculpture… depart[ing] from the legitimate provenance of the needle', and judged the technique to be unworthy of detailed consideration in his chapter on the seventeenth century.[41] The renowned scholar and practitioner Grace Christie (1872–1953) was equally exercised by this issue: 'stump work' was the 'wrong kind' of relief compared with the 'temperance and judgment' of fourteenth-century needlework.[42] To further reinforce this point, some critics drew on continental embroidery. May Morris, for instance, even cited seventeenth-century Spanish raised work, a medium that she despised intensely, but thought 'comparatively sane' next to the 'riotous nonsense' of English raised embroidery.[43]

Fig. 2.6
Embroidered picture, *Two ladies personifying Taste and Touch* (?), third quarter of the seventeenth century, detail, Metropolitan Museum of Art 64.101.1337. © Metropolitan Museum of Art, New York.

Finally, commentators condescendingly remarked on the multifarious items made to satisfy the demands of Stuart needlewomen. *The Art Journal*, for instance, noted the excesses of some workers who plastered their embroideries with glass, coral and metal 'till a magpie might have purveyed the materials' (Fig. 2.6).[44] Mary Symonds and Louisa Preece in their comprehensive survey *Needlework through the ages* (1928), were intrigued by the myriad threads, beads and semi-precious stones found in seventeenth-century raised work, but ultimately questioned their artistic merit:

> The ingenuity of the embroiderer in working up their materials into such decoration... and the fine technique are amazing, so that we may be deceived into admiration as with the beautiful language of a writer or speaker whose subject makes no appeal. Curious, not beautiful, and in its artificiality missing the real spirit of art, it is not surprising that stump work was so short-lived and did not in Europe survive the century.[45]

Nevertheless, despite the scorn heaped upon it, English raised work would still undergo a partial renascence in the hands of a select few embroiderers during this period.

The revival of 'stump work'

When the *Dictionary of Needlework* was published in 1882, Saward was correct in noting that 'Embroidery on the stamp... has no counterpart in modern times'.[46] The fashion for raised work in the home had petered out by the early 1700s; however, by the late nineteenth century this had begun to change. Women's journals and needlework magazines promoting the practice of art embroidery very occasionally featured historic specimens in the belief that the best way to learn was to study old masterpieces.[47] In February 1891, *The Queen* ran a two-page spread on Ann Greenhill's 1677 workbox (Fig. 2.7), which belonged to one of the RSAN's founding members, Lady Charlotte Schreiber, describing it as 'an excellent example of this curious old work'.[48] Likewise, the May 1912 issue of *Needlecraft Monthly Magazine* dedicated its series 'Triumphs of Embroidery' to Hannah Smith's 1656 casket, which incorporated a small amount of padding on the lid.[49] Nonetheless, the author concluded that it was unlikely any worker would attempt such an undertaking, given the amount of time and effort required to produce something similar.[50] Kendrick reiterated the point eighteen months later: '... however curious and attractive in detail, [it] is not likely to be flattered with extensive imitation in our own day.'[51]

Whilst modern 'stump work' does not feature in the pages of embroidery manuals or decorative needlework magazines published in the late nineteenth and early twentieth centuries,[52] it did enjoy a following, albeit a very limited one. The press attributed this revival to the RSAN and its superintendent, Louisa Wade, who had mastered the technique by the early 1900s.[53] Having been commissioned from the outset to repair and transfer antique needlework, the School was familiar with

Stuart raised or 'padded' embroidery. Specimens regularly appeared in its loan exhibitions,[54] or were offered for sale through the showroom, as in the case of Viscountess Wolesley's collection of needlework pictures and caskets.[55] Charged with the task of keeping historic stitch alive,[56] the RSAN also collected examples of old work from which copies were made and bound into reference books. These were stored in display cases in the various workrooms in the hope of inspiring future generations of designers and embroiderers.

By the turn of the nineteenth century, the RSAN had emerged as the forerunner in the production of replicas of ancient needlework, particularly crewel embroidery in the Jacobean style. These were sold as kits or one-off commissions, and many examples can be found in public and private collections. Yet, specimens of 'stump work' from the period are rare. It may be that some pieces have been wrongly or indeed wilfully misattributed to the seventeenth century as Stuart raised embroidery became more and more a collector's item and its monetary value increased.[57] One such example is the panel *Abigail and David*, sold to the collector William Hesketh Lever in 1920. At the time of its acquisition, it was said to date from around 1680, but the panel, which is more akin to a Victorian shadow box, appears to be a late nineteenth-century imitation of a raised work picture.[58] Even so, misattribution was not the norm and cannot account for the paucity of examples dating from this period. It is more likely that the apparent flaws of 'stump work' prevented it from overcoming the influence of art embroidery designers and teachers who were inclined to dismiss it. That being said, there were some rare exceptions, a handful of which are discussed below.

Fig. 2.7
Workbox embroidered by Ann Greenhill, 1677, formerly in the collection of Lady Charlotte Schreiber (1834-1922).
© Bonhams.

Between 1907 and 1913, *Needlecraft Monthly Magazine* ran a series of articles entitled 'Notable Needleworkers', which showcased over fifty women whose embroideries were well-known to the public through articles printed in the daily press and in society magazines like *The Queen* and *The Ladies Field*, as well as through exhibitions hosted by the Royal Amateur Art Society and the Athene Society of Broderers. Both London-based institutions acted as a barometer of taste, at least among the middle and upper classes. It is telling that only one 'Notable Needleworker' – Lucy Studdy (1847–1928) – is known to have tackled raised work prior to the First World War.[59] Among the many pieces displayed in the drawing room of her home Avenue House, Bishopton, Stratford-upon-Avon, was a casket stitched in 'the manner of Stuart stump embroideries' (Fig. 2.8), described by the magazine's editor as 'so admirably faithful to the feeling of the old models that it has often been mistaken for a genuine antique'.[60] The lid featured a woman in seventeenth-century dress surrounded by motifs commonly found in historic raised work. Depicted on the front panel was the façade of Studdy's former home,

Fig. 2.8
'Casket of stump embroidery in Stuart style worked by Mrs Studdy', *Needlecraft Monthly Magazine,* vol. 3, no. 9 (September 1909), p. 302. © Photo Lynn Hulse.

Fig. 2.9a–b (see overleaf)
Details from the mirror frame worked by Leonora Jenner for Avebury Manor, Wiltshire, c. 1916. © Photos Lynn Hulse, reproduced with permission of the National Trust.

Fig. 2.9b

the sixteenth-century manor house Clifford Chambers. In a departure from 'the old style', the background was painted in a mode typical of needlework pictures of the early 1900s.[61]

One notable exception to the limited vogue for 'stump work' displayed by early twentieth-century embroiderers was Leonora Jenner (1869–1952), whose output comprised at least two caskets,[62] two picture panels[63] and two mirror frames.[64] Her passion for raised embroidery in the Stuart style is thought to have developed in the course of restoring the interior of Avebury Manor, the Tudor house in Wiltshire where she and her second husband lived between 1902 and 1935. Much of Jenner's work was completed immediately after the period under review; however, a newspaper cutting dating from 1916 found within the mirror frame on display at Avebury suggests that this embroidery may in fact date from the First World War. The execution of the male and female figures together with the flora and fauna, stitched in a variety of threads and novelty items, is testament to Jenner's consummate skill in emulating seventeenth-century raised work and hints at the possibility that she was taught by the RSAN (Fig. 2.9a-b).

While a faithful revival of Stuart raised work failed to gain major traction among embroiderers, various attempts were made in the early 1910s to update the technique in order to make it more fashionable and relevant. According to *The Pall Mall Gazette*, 'Patriotic people having a *penchant* in this direction modernise the old idea of embroidering a picture of a modern king and queen, with suitable

Fig. 2.10
'Stump work'
panel of Sir
Richard Paget,
Lady Paget and
their family,
1901–1927,
reproduced in
The Sketch, 4
April 1934, p. 15.
© Mary Evans
Picture Library.

surroundings. Even one's own family history would be interesting to descendants if carried out in the same way.'[65] Nonetheless, with a few exceptions these efforts would also falter. One such example was an elaborate needlework picture of Sir Richard and Lady Caroline Paget (1848–1946) with their children and grandchildren seated below the arcade of their family home at Cranmore Hall near Shepton Mallet in Somerset (Fig. 2.10). Worked between 1901 and 1927, the embroidery was inspired by a raised work picture stitched by Paget's ancestor, Mary Ruddock, in 1683. Paget's son Richard designed the Edwardian panel and modelled the faces and hands in plaster-of-Paris, which was later waxed and painted over. Lady Paget embroidered all the architectural details and the leaves, and each of the ladies in the group stitched her own costume.[66]

Conclusion

The response of many late nineteenth- and early twentieth-century scholars and practitioners to raised work was ambivalent at best, scathing at worst; 'in its English form,' wrote Rachel Head, '[it] is without doubt the most grotesque and eccentric of any sort of decorative stitchery ever conceived and executed. It is entirely without artistic merit'.[67] This sentiment succinctly encapsulated the major issues that contemporary commentators and embroiderers had with Stuart raised work. Not only was the intricacy of the work highly contentious but, more significantly, the medium ignored the medieval principles on which good design and art embroidery itself were based. These principles dominated the values and aesthetics of the Arts and Crafts movement and underpinned its belief that, in its highest form, embroidery was not merely a craft but 'belonged to the sacred ranks of what are called works of art'.[68] The RSAN's efforts to popularise the technique met with very little success, and those examples that have come to light were, like their seventeenth-century antecedents, made primarily by middle and upper class women with both the time and financial means to indulge their "eccentric" interest.

Due perhaps to the values and lingering prejudices of art embroiderers, 'stump work' would remain on the fringes of embroidery practice well into the twentieth century and continue to divide critics as to its aesthetic and artistic merit. Whether Stuart raised work deserved the blistering critique it received may ultimately rest on one's appreciation of the technique itself; as one observer wryly pronounced, 'In matters of art there [is] no single canon of beauty. What was exquisite to one person might not be to another. In matters of art they must be their own interpreters.'[69]

Notes

[1] Frank Davis, 'A Page for Collectors: French 17th Century Needlework', *The Illustrated London News,* 11 August 1934, p. 234.

[2] 'Stump-work', *The Pall Mall Gazette,* 5 March 1912, p. 12.

[3] Mary M. Brooks, '"Another freak of fashion": Collectors, collecting, connoisseurship and changing views of 17th century English embroideries', *Text,* vol. 39 (2011–12), pp. 12–17.

[4] The School of Art Needlework acquired its royal prefix in March 1875. The word 'Art' was dropped from the title in 1922.

[5] The Museum was renamed the Victoria and Albert (V&A) in 1899. *Catalogue of the Special Loan Exhibition of Decorative Art Needlework made before 1800* (London: Printed at the Chiswick Press, 1874), pp. v-vi (revised and illustrated edition of the 1873 catalogue).

[6] Op. cit., p. v.

[7] Op. cit., pp. vii-viii; see, for example, *The Pall Mall Gazette,* 15 April 1873, p. 14.

[8] See, for example, London, V&A, 892-1864, *Esther and Ahasuerus,* English, 1660–1690, described as 'a piece of silk embroidery... worked in high relief'; Daniel Rock, *Textile Fabrics* (London: Chapman and Hall, 1870), p. 319.

[9] *Catalogue,* no. 193. Described by the art dealer Sidney Hand as 'undoubtedly one of the finest caskets in existence', the box has been attributed to Elizabeth Coombe ('The lost art of the needle: petit-point; "stump" and bead work', *Illustrated London News,* 29 May 1920, p. 927). The work was subsequently acquired by the V&A (T.43-1954).

[10] See, for example, *Catalogue,* nos 189, 192, 193, 203, 208, 210A and 211.

[11] Fol. [A4] and The Third Book, p. 98 respectively.

[12] S. F. A. Caulfeild and B. C. Saward, *The Dictionary of Needlework* (London: L. Upcott Gill, 1882), p. 172; 2nd edn (London: A. W. Cowan, 1887), pp. 171-172. Blanche Saward was responsible for the sections on church embroidery, lace and ornamental needlework.

[13] See, for example, Mrs Head, 'English Secular Embroidery of the Sixteenth and Seventeenth Centuries', *The Burlington Magazine,* vol. IV/11 (February 1904), pp. 168-175, at p. 173 and Kay Dennis, *Beginner's Guide to Stumpwork* (Tunbridge Wells: Search Press Ltd, 2001), p. 8.

[14] John L. Nevinson, *Catalogue of English Domestic Embroidery of the Sixteenth & Seventeenth Centuries* (London: HMSO, 1938), p. xxi.

[15] 'Special Loan Exhibition of Decorative Needlework at South Kensington', *The Queen*, 19 April 1873, p. 307.

[16] John Piggott, 'Ancient Embroidery', *The Art Journal*, 1873, pp. 263-264, at p. 264.

[17] Head, 'English Secular Embroidery of the Sixteenth and Seventeenth Centuries', p. 173.

[18] 'Stuart Embroideries', *The Art Journal* (1904), pp. 234-235, at p. 234; 'Curious Embroideries and Pictures in Needlework', *The Pall Mall Gazette*, 17 July 1902, p. 2; 'Stump-Work', p. 12.

[19] Doris Moxon, 'The History of Animals in Embroidery', *The Embroideress*, no. 7 (August 1923), p. 163; May Morris, 'Embroidery', in Board of Trade, *Ghent International Exhibition 1913: Catalogue of the British Arts and Crafts Exhibition Section* (London: Board of Trade Exhibitions Branch, 1913), pp. clxii-clxxvii, at p. clxx; 'Art Treasures', *The Scotsman*, 12 October 1932, p. 12; May Morris, 'Of Church Embroidery IV: Couching and Raised Gold -Work', *The Building News*, 65 (1893), pp. 674-675, at p. 675.

[20] Therle Hughes, *English Domestic Needlework 1660-1860* (London: Abbey Fine Arts, 1961), p. 164.

[21] See, for example, May Morris, *Decorative Needlework* (London: Joseph Hughes & Co., 1893), p. 79.

[22] Piggott, 'Ancient Embroidery', p. 264. It was not uncommon at this time for 'stump work' to be mistakingly dated to the sixteenth century.

[23] Lady Marian Alford, *Needlework as Art* (London: Sampson Low, Marston, Searle, and Rivington, 1886), p. 390. The Fishmonger's pall (1512–c. 1538) was included in the *Special Loan Exhibition* among 'Works of all kinds having historical interest', where it was incorrectly dated to the late fourteenth century, *Catalogue*, no. 53; see also Clare Browne, Glyn Davies and M. A. Michael, eds, *English Medieval Embroidery: Opus Anglicanum* (New Haven & London: Yale University Press, 2016), pp. 272-274. The Dunstable or Fayrey pall (c. 1470–1530) was displayed at the RSAN in Spring 1881; *Catalogue of The Special Exhibition of Ancient English and Other Art Needlework made before 1800* (London, 1881), no. 24. The pall is currently on long-term loan to the V&A (LOAN:ST.PETER.2) and is on display in the British Galleries.

[24] Cole, 'Some Aspects of Ancient and Modern Embroidery: Lecture II', *Journal of the Society of Arts*, vol. 53, no. 2752 (18 August 1905), pp. 973-984, at p. 980, referring to the casket V&A 1070-1873. See, for example, the Sherborne missal, London, British Library, Add. MS 74236.

[25] Morris, 'Church Embroidery IV', p. 675; 'The Exhibition of Art Needlework', *The Queen*, 14 June 1873, p. 476.

[26] Ellen T. Masters, *The Gentlewoman's Book of Art Needlework* (London: Henry & Co., 1893), p. 48.

[27] V&A 125-1878; Morris, 'Of Church Embroidery IV', p. 675.

[28] Margaret Jourdain, *The History of English Secular Embroidery* (London: K. Paul, Trench, Trèubner & Co., 1910), p. 161. This view was reiterated a generation later by Mary Thomas; *Embroidery Book* (London: Hodder & Stoughton, 1936), p. 262.

[29] Selwyn Image, 'On Designing for the Art of Embroidery', *Arts and Crafts Essays* (London: Rivington, Percival, Co., 1893), pp. 414-420, at p. 417.

[30] William Morris Gallery, London, J561vii, May Morris, Notes and sketches for embroidery lectures, c. 1899–1902.

[31] The Marshalls ascribed these anomalies to the Reformation and its impact on religious iconography, where everything connected with 'the old superstition' had been swept aside; Frances and Hugh Marshall, *Old English Embroidery: its Technique and Symbolism* (London: Horace Cox, 1894), p. 96.

[32] 'Stuart Embroideries', p. 234.

[33] Alford, *Needlework as Art*, p. 389; Thomas, *Embroidery Book*, p. 262.

[34] Morris, 'Of Church Embroidery IV', p. 675.

[35] Marshall & Marshall, *Old English Embroidery*, p. 98.

[36] A. J. B. Wace, 'My Lady's Trinket Box: Stuart Needlework Caskets', *Illustrated London News*, 10 March 1928, p. 388.

[37] Eugenie Gibson, 'Mr Percival D. Griffiths' Collection of Old English Needlework', Part II, *The Connoisseur*, vol. 59 (January–April 1921), pp. 153-158, at pp. 153-154.

[38] Mrs Head, *The Lace and Embroidery Collector* (London: Herbert Jenkins Ltd, 1922), p. 174. See also Mary Symonds (Mrs Guy Antrobus) and Louisa Preece, *Needlework through the ages: a short survey of its development in decorative art, with particular regard to its inspirational relationship with other methods of craftsmanship* (London: Hodder & Stoughton Ltd, 1928), p. 270.

[39] 'Stuart Embroideries', p. 234.

[40] Elizabeth Glaister, *Needlework* (London: Macmillan & Co., 1880), p. 26.

41 A. F. Kendrick, *English Embroidery* (London: George Newnes Ltd/ New York: Charles Scribner's Sons, 1905), p. 92.

42 Mrs Grace Christie, *Embroidery & Tapestry Weaving* (London: John Hogg, 1906), pp. 192-193.

43 Morris, 'Of Church Embroidery IV', p. 675.

44 'Stuart Embroideries', p. 234.

45 Symonds and Preece, *Needlework through the ages*, p. 283.

46 Caulfeild and Saward, *The Dictionary of Needlework,* p. 172.

47 See, for example, the series 'Triumphs of Embroidery' in *Needlecraft Monthly Magazine,* vols 5-6 (1911–1912).

48 *The Queen,* 7 February 1891, pp. 210-211. The workbox was recently sold at Bonhams in the sale *Fine English Furniture and Works of Art including the Richmond Collection of Early English Needlework,* 2 March 2011, lot 16.

49 The University of Manchester The Whitworth, Hannah Smith's casket, 1654–1656, T.8237.1.

50 'Triumphs of Embroidery no. 8', *Needlecraft Monthly Magazine,* vol. 6, no. 5 (May 1912), pp. 125-127, at p. 127.

51 A. F. Kendrick, 'Prefatory note', *Catalogue of an Exhibition of British Needlework from the 16th Century Onward* (Hastings: F. J. Parsons, October 1913), n. p.

52 See, for example, *Needlecraft Monthly Magazine, Embroidery, Needle and Thread, Needlecraft Practical Journal, Weldon's Practical Needlework, Fancy Needlework Illustrated* and *The Embroideress*.

53 'Art in Needlework', *The Pall Mall Gazette,* 25 September 1920, p. 6; 'Art and Literature', *Diss Express,* 6 May 1904, p. 3.

54 See, for example, *Catalogue of the Special Exhibition... made before 1800,* nos 100 and 145.

55 'Stuart Embroideries', p. 234.

56 'Handbook of Embroidery', *The Queen,* 7 February 1880, p. 121.

57 Brooks, '"Another freak of fashion"', pp. 14-16; Emily Lowes, *Chats on Old Lace and Needlework* (London: T. Fisher Unwin, 1908), pp. 270-273.

58 Xanthe Brooke, *The Lady Lever Art Gallery Catalogue of Embroideries* (Stroud: Alan Sutton Publishing Ltd, 1992), p. 86, LL5284. For another late nineteenth-century raised work panel on the same theme, see Sonia O'Connor, 'Image interpretation', in *X-radiography of Textiles, Dress and Related Objects,* edited by Sonia A. O'Connor and Mary M. Brooks (Oxford: Elsevier, 2007), pp. 74-90, at pp. 83-84 and Brooks, '"Another freak of fashion"', pp. 15-16.

59 'Notable Needleworkers', second series, no. 9, *Needlecraft Monthly Magazine,* vol. 3, no. 9 (September 1909), pp. 301-304. Lady Jane Cory, whose work featured in the first issue of the series (vol. 1, no. 4, July 1907, pp. 115-117), stitched a raised work casket with the help of the RSAN in 1920–1921. For more information, see Lynn Hulse, *The Embroidered Furnishings of the Lethbridge Sisters, c. 1899–1928* (London: OE Publications, forthcoming).

60 'Notable Needleworkers', p. 302.

61 Ibid.

62 *Christies Costume and Textiles,* 15 March 2005, lot no. 191, casket signed and dated 'Leonora Jenner 1940'; http://needleprint.blogspot.com/2011/09/mrs-jenners-casket.html - see also comments dated 16 and 18 December 2011 [accessed 2 July 2018]. The second casket is dated '1936–1937'.

63 *Christies Interiors – Masters and Makers,* 2 December 2014, lot no. 441, c. 1940; http://thistle-threads.blogspot.co.uk/2014/11/another-lamora-jenner.html (*sic*); Bath, Holburne Museum, accession no. T2008.259, c. 1940.

64 Avebury Manor National Trust, NT 220753, and Lytes Cary Manor National Trust, NT 254756. The latter is thought to be the work of both Leonora and her sister, Flora, who was also an accomplished needlewoman.

65 'Stump-Work', p. 12.

66 '"Family Portrait" Stitchery: Paget Stump-Work', *The Sketch,* 4 April 1934, p. 15.

67 Head, *The Lace and Embroidery Collector,* p. 174.

68 May Morris, 'Mediæval Embroidery', *The Journal of the Society of Arts,* vol. 43, no. 2207 (8 March 1895), pp. 384-396, at p. 388.

69 'Notts. Art Exhibition "of Exquisite Beauty"', *Nottingham Journal,* 6 May 1937, p. 4.

3   The language of stitch
Jacqui Carey

There has been a long-standing interest in historic English embroidery, and today many surviving examples can be found preserved in museum collections. In most respects, these artefacts have physically remained the same, but their interpretation has changed over time, reflecting opinions and attitudes of the period. Publications provide a wealth of information, with images and text discussing the objects and their background context, yet details about the stitches are often lacking or vague. Moreover, recent object-based research has revealed that many stitches have long been misidentified in written material.[1]

Stitches are the key feature that differentiates embroidery from other historic artefacts, and they have the potential to tell us much about past practice. As a consequence, any misreading of the extant material impacts on our understanding and carries the risk of undermining any ideas based on its classification. Historians acknowledge the importance of returning to a text's original source rather than depending on transcriptions or secondary material.[2] Thus, it seems timely that we reassess our examination of the actual stitches rather than rely on the well-repeated text-based information that accompanies them. Historians also recognise that it is 'difficult to do away with a wrong identification',[3] especially in light of the dominance of text that tends to give the 'written word priority over physical evidence'.[4]

In addition to mistaken identity, research is uncovering many stitches that have become obsolete. For instance, during a detailed survey of thirty-five sweet bags, a total of fifty-seven different types of decorative stitch were discovered, yet only eleven of these could be found in modern publications. Subsequent analysis is unearthing similar statistics on different types of embroidered items.[5] By studying other surviving examples, much more will undoubtedly be discovered, yet accessing a narrative from these mute objects can be a problem.

Henry Glassie argues that literacy was not commonplace, and that objects are a more representative source of information than words.[6] Whilst there is no shortage of written material dating from the seventeenth century, it is accepted that extant embroidery can be utilised as a means of accessing the unspoken, thus adding more depth to our knowledge, particularly concerning the female domestic domain.[7] Nevertheless, the physicality of the stitches still tends to be overlooked. This may be because, unlike attributes such as design or iconography, the constructional components of stitching are difficult to research at a distance. Like any language, the stitches need to be seen before they can be understood and interpreted. Unfortunately, observing them with clarity is challenging because of the small scale of the stitches. Furthermore, their often-fragile nature creates a dilemma for museum custodians as they try to balance between making an object available for study and preserving its integrity.[8] Adding to issues of accessibility are time and financial constraints since working from original material can be painfully slow to interpret.[9] In spite of the challenges, the use of close-up photography has greatly enhanced our ability to examine stitches in detail. However, as a secondary source these should be treated with caution; as Georgios Boudalis points out, 'photography usually makes no distinction between what is important and what is not'.[10] Be that as it may, even when images clearly illustrate the stitches, contradictions exist within the accompanying text. This suggests that there is also an issue with understanding the language of stitch: in order to read the material it needs to be both seen and recognised.

Today, we take reading text for granted. The black marks on this page are so commonplace that they do not require explanation. There is a collective and implicit agreement that these marks make words that can be "taken as read", and from them we come to some shared understanding. Nonetheless, this has not always been the case, and we often forget the complexity of this learnt behaviour and cultural doctrine. Gaining skill in any form of language involves the recognition of the symbols, and learning the accepted classification system that identifies "same" and "different". For instance, our mutual and embedded knowledge allows us to read Fig. 3.1 not as a circle joined to a straight line, but as the letter 'b'. Intriguingly, we also recognise the same symbol in Fig. 3.2, in spite of the changes in colour, size and shape. Yet, the seemingly similar circle and straight line shown in Fig. 3.3 are discerned as the distinctly different letter 'd'. Such comprehension has

Fig. 3.1   Fig. 3.2   Fig. 3.3

been achieved with a great deal of practice; however, the ability to understand is given little consideration because it is usually undertaken during childhood and the memory of it recedes, though the experience can be readily appreciated when faced with learning any unknown non-Roman writing system.

Whilst today's embroiderers may be fluent in their stitching, this is not always an advantage when it comes to reading historic stitches. As Hoffmann explains, 'If you know how it should be, you may see what you expect to see'.[11] Indeed, it seems likely that this has been the cause of many mistaken identities; they are usually mislabelled as a well-known stitch practised today, which looks similar to the historic one. This suggests that the interpreter is familiar with modern embroidery but unaware of differences in the language of historic stitches, much like the uninitiated mistaking a 'long s' for an 'f' in old text (Fig. 3.4).

As with any language, the form of the symbols can be learnt, so that each historic stitch may be differentiated and named. Unfortunately, stitch terminology is not standardised; several names are commonly attributed to one stitch, or the same term ascribed to several different stitches. Therefore, although stitch names found in seventeenth-century documentation have filtered down through time, these cannot be accurately attributed to the extant examples.[12] Nevertheless, today's dictionaries, encyclopaedias and other sources act as vital tools, helping to pinpoint a reference that can illustrate how one chooses to define a selected term. There is an abundance of this kind of material, removing the need for any ambiguity (Fig. 3.5). However, these resources may be somewhat lacking, even when they profess to advise on historic material. The omission of so many historic stitches is a setback for anyone searching for the unfamiliar. Although of greater concern is the mass of misleading assertions made about the form of historic English embroidery, as these compound the problem by setting a precedent for the novice reader of historic stitches. Unfortunately, this situation has been perpetuated for over a century, embedding an expectation about what one will find when looking at old needlework. Furthermore, the misunderstanding about historic stitches has been re-enforced with authoritative texts that erroneously connect specific examples of extant embroidery to the current lexicon.

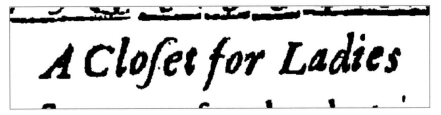

Fig. 3.4
An example of historic writing using a 'long s' that looks like a modern letter 'f'.
© Photo Jacqui Carey.

Fig. 3.5
A selection of the many reference books that can be used to define stitch terminology.
© Photo Jacqui Carey.

Interest in seventeenth-century English embroidery, coupled with recent revelations about historic stitches, is starting to turn the tide of misconceptions and increasing the call for the material to be reviewed. With the recognition that the artefact, rather than the accompanying text, may be the more reliable source for historic stitches comes a need for what Linda Hurcombe calls 'a specialist in the craft of finds analysis.'[13] Like any craft, this skill is best learnt through repeated practice. While a practical understanding of embroidery is helpful, the skill has more to do with 'physical analysis, textural recognition of key features and the knowledge base to reject certain possible causes and accept others.'[14] With this in mind, it can be useful to learn from the analysis of woven artefacts. Here, the tendency is to establish the structure of a fabric before considering the technique that may have produced it. This is because structure is a physical attribute that can be determined, while technique is an action and intangible. As Irene Emery says, '... *structure* inheres in the fabric... whereas evidence of *process* is seldom retained.'[15] Furthermore, it is accepted that there are often many alternative ways of making the same structure.[16]

The relationship between structure and technique is illustrated in Fig. 3.6, and highlights that one particular structure can be made using several different techniques, but a specific technique[17] only results in one structure. Let's explore this in relation to embroidery by using the example of chain stitch (Fig. 3.7). Its structure is unequivocal and is depicted in the stylised diagram shown in Fig. 3.8. However, deciding on how this particular example was made is more problematic; there are three well-known specific techniques (Fig. 3.9a, b & c) that could have produced this structure, as well as the potential for other less obvious ways of working. As a result of this correlation between process and product, it is possible to identify a stitch structure by examining a historic artefact, but determining how it was made is open to debate. Along with other textile analysis, building up the case for one method over another tends to be

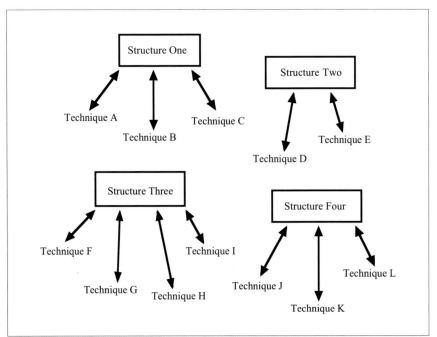

Fig. 3.6
The relationship between structures and techniques.
© Jacqui Carey.

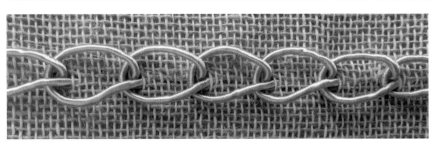

Fig. 3.7
Chain stitch.
© Jacqui Carey.

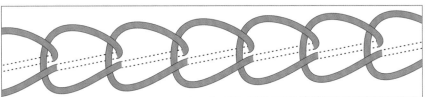

Fig. 3.8
Diagram illustrating the structure of chain stitch.
© Jacqui Carey.

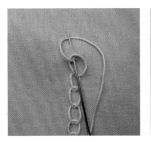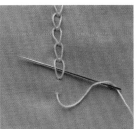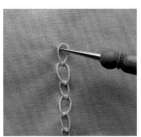

Fig. 3.9a, b & c
Three different techniques that can be used to make the structure of chain stitch.
© Jacqui Carey.

based on supporting contextual material, likelihoods suggested by small detail, practical experiment and personal opinion.

In contrast, while uncertainty surrounds how a historic stitch was worked, one can reliably say how it was not made and specific techniques categorically dismissed. For instance, Technique A cannot be used to produce Structure Two in Fig. 3.6, while the techniques shown in Fig. 3.9a, b & c will never produce the stitch illustrated in Fig. 3.10. As a consequence of the single outcome generated from a specific technique, one can be in no doubt about rejecting much of the conventional view found in the text-based identification of historic stitches. Here, an assumed technique may be discounted since it does not produce the stitch structure found on the artefact.

It is clear that because of its definitive nature, stitch structure plays a significant role in object-based research, much like the alphabet of a language. Learning to read historic stitches in this way opens up the "text", allowing us to read the evidence of past practice, and reveals a fascinating comparison to modern practice. Inevitably the extant material raises lots of questions. For example, when and why did some stitches become obsolete? What can differences in stitch tell us about the chronological or geographical spread of practical knowledge? Furthermore, revisiting well-known artefacts stimulates broader enquiry, such as why has there been a difference in interpretation and how has textile research developed?

While the analytical process of stitch identification is a fundamental part of reading historic embroidery, the intangible techniques offer intrigue and debate. Moreover, they open up the potential to engage with the past through practical recreation. Jules Prown was keen to advocate the importance of investigating the relationship between artefact and perceiver. He divided the process into three parts: 'Sensory engagement... Intellectual engagement... Emotional response'.[18] Considering an artefact in this manner will vary depending on the individual: everyone approaches an object with a unique set of personal experiences, which can influence their response. In this context, modern embroiderers are in the privileged position of being able to make connections with both the noun and the verb of seventeenth-century embroidered work. Practice generates a tacit and embodied knowledge

Fig. 3.10
Elizabethan holly braid stitch.
© Jacqui Carey.

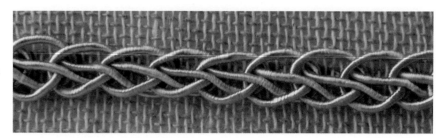

that cannot be readily gained through theory.[19] This extra dimension adds depth to a maker's interpretation of the narrative contained within these mute artefacts because practice connects both the objects and the embroiderers from the past. Stitch structure provides an alphabet that is manipulated through technique. Thus, the process of recreating objects offers a means of engaging with history in a visceral way, allowing embroiderers to relate to the stories of challenge and triumph that transcend the spelling and grammar of stitches.

Notes

[1] Comparisons between reoccurring text-based statements and the stitches identified by this author's examination of extant examples can be found in Jacqui Carey, *Sweet Bags: An Investigation into 16th & 17th Century Needlework* (Ottery St Mary: Carey Company, 2009); idem, *Elizabethan Stitches: A Guide to Historic English Needlework* (Ottery St Mary: Carey Company, 2012).

[2] John Tosh and Sean Lang, *The Pursuit of History: Aims, Methods, and New Directions in the Study of Modern History,* 4th edn (New York: Longman, 2006), p. 60.

[3] Marta Hoffmann, 'Textile implements: identification in archaeological finds and interpretation in pictorial sources', in *Archaeological Textiles: Report from the 2nd NESAT Symposium, May 1-4, 1984,* edited by Lise Bender Jørgensen, Bente Magnus and Elisabeth Munksgaard (Copenhagen: Arkaeologisk Institut, 1988), pp. 232-246, at p. 233.

[4] Kevin Greene, *Archaeology: An Introduction* (London: Routledge, 2002), p. 2.

[5] These statistics do not include couched work or functional sewing stitches, and are based on the author's unpublished database, which is limited to items that she has analysed.

[6] Jules David Prown, 'Mind in matter: an introduction to material culture theory and method', *Winterthur Portfolio,* vol. 17, no. 1 (1982), pp. 1-19, at p. 3.

[7] See for example, Rozsika Parker, *The Subversive Stitch: Embroidery and the Making of the Feminine* (London: Women's Press, 1988; rev. edn, London: I. B. Tauris & Co. Ltd, 2010) and Susan Frye, *Pens and Needles: Women's Textualities in Early Modern England* (Philadelphia: University of Pennsylvania Press, 2010).

[8] For more discussion, see Mary Brooks, Alison Lister, Dinah Eastop and Tarja Bennett, 'Artifact or Information? Articulating the Conflicts in Conserving Archaeological Textiles', in *Archaeological Conservation and Its Consequences. Preprints of the Contributions to the Copenhagen Congress, 26–30 August 1996,* edited by Ashok Roy and Perry Smith (London: The International Institute for Conservation of Historic and Artistic Works, 1996), pp. 16-21.

[9] Tosh, *The Pursuit of History,* p. 91, and attested to by this author's own experience.

[10] Georgios Boudalis, 'A Drawing Is Worth a Thousand Words', *ICON News,* vol. 11, (2015), pp.11-13, at p. 11.

[11] Hoffmann, 'Textile implements', p. 242.

[12] See Carey, *Sweet Bags,* p. 66 for more detail, and the stitch names from two of the best-known sources: Randle Holme, *The Academy of Armory, or, A Storehouse of Armory and Blazon* (Chester: Printed for the Author, 1688), and John Taylor, *The Needles Excellency. A New Booke wherein are divers Admirable Workes wrought with the Needle,* 12th edn (London: Printed for James Boler, 1640).

[13] Linda Hurcombe, *Archaeological Artefacts as Material Culture* (Abingdon: Routledge, 2007), p. 36.

[14] Ibid.

[15] Irene Emery, *The Primary Structure of Fabrics: An Illustrated Classification,* 3rd edn (London: Thames and Hudson, 1994), p. xv.

[16] Annemarie Seiler-Baldinger, *Textiles: A Classification of Techniques* (Bathurst, N. S. W.: Crawford House Press, 1994), p. xv.

[17] Here the term 'specific technique' is used to describe a set of unvarying repeated actions, as opposed to a 'generic technique', which covers a style of work, such as embroidery.

[18] Prown, 'Mind in matter', pp. 8-9.

[19] See, for example, Peter Dormer, *The Art of the Maker* (London: Thames & Hudson, 1994).

4 Degradation and preservation: the consequences of age and use in seventeenth-century English embroideries from the collection of the Ashmolean Museum, Oxford

Susan M. Stanton

In 2017, the Ashmolean Museum hosted a temporary display of fifteen newly created caskets made in the style of seventeenth-century English raised work. The contrast between these new creations and the original seventeenth-century pieces in the Ashmolean's own collection provided a striking reminder of how objects change over time. This paper examines the nature of these changes, looks at the factors that caused them to occur and outlines the measures conservators undertake to promote the preservation of these fascinating pieces.

One of the treasures in the Museum's textile collection is a box embroidered with scenes from the life of Abraham, dating from before 1665. Fig. 4.1a & b shows a side panel of the lid alongside one of the new boxes in the 2017 display.[1] These two embroideries were created over 350 years apart but the techniques and materials used are similar. Except for the muted colours and dull metal threads of the older piece, their appearance remains very close.

Materials and techniques

Makers have employed an impressive range of materials to achieve the details, textures and luxurious effects characteristic of this type of needlework. The ground fabric of the seventeenth-century works tends to be either a light coloured silk satin or a canvas completely covered with silk or metal thread stitching. The various applied elements include materials acquired specifically for embroidery and also items found around the home environment of the stitcher. There are numerous types of silk and metal thread, pearls, spangles, coral and glass beads. Fragments of the shiny mineral mica are used for windows and mirrors, while the figures' hairstyles are sometimes made of real hair. Iridescent feathers are often used in the decoration of the insects and caterpillars, which are frequently found in the designs. More unusual elements in the Ashmolean's collection of embroideries include a small avian skull, which forms the base for an embroidered bird's head,[2] and possibly the shaft of a feather used as a water pipe.[3] Three-dimensional features are achieved with under-pads of fibre, fabric or wood,[4] and detached needle lace elements can be stiffened with wire and paper to raise and accentuate parts of the design. This range of materials will all have an impact on how the objects change and deteriorate over time. The different physical and chemical properties of the materials react in individual ways to the conditions encountered by the embroideries through use and the passage of time.

Fig. 4.1a
Box, *Scenes from the life of Abraham*, before 1665, detail, WA 1947.191.315. Image © Ashmolean Museum, University of Oxford.

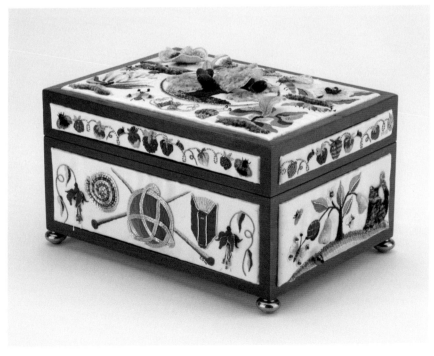

Fig. 4.1b
Casket designed by Nicola Jarvis and embroidered by Ann Stainton, 2017. © Photo David Gowers.

49

Condition of seventeenth-century embroideries

The pre-1665 box referred to above (Fig. 4.1a) is a remarkable survivor and its fine condition is exceptional among collections of seventeenth-century embroideries. Its physical state can also deceive the viewer into thinking that the box is stronger and more resilient than other pieces from the same period, which are more obviously damaged. The cream satin fabric retains its fine silk warp fibres but over time they have become very fragile. This was evident when gentle conservation cleaning was attempted under a microscope with a fine brush and low-power vacuum suction (LPVS). The warp fibres could be seen to fragment into dust under the light brush strokes and surface cleaning was not continued.

Another box in the Ashmolean collection, the Kiel casket, displays more typical condition for textiles surviving from the seventeenth century. Fig. 4.2a shows an image of the lid of this casket, which graphically illustrates what frequently happens to this type of embroidery over time. The face of the fashionably dressed male figure measures approximately 20mm from top to bottom, and when photographed through a microscope the detail of the damage is revealed (Fig. 4.2b). The cream satin fabric over the nose is completely lost, exposing the white fibre under-padding. On the forehead and right cheek the fine silk warp threads of the satin have also been lost, leaving only the weft threads, and therefore a fabric with no structural integrity. In addition, the coloured silk embroidery threads used

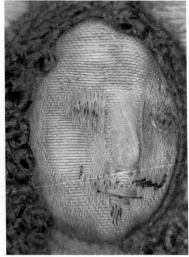

Fig. 4.2a
Keil casket, detail of figure on lid, c. 1670, WA 2017.37. Image © Ashmolean Museum, University of Oxford.

Fig. 4.2b
Keil casket, detail of face of figure on lid, c. 1670. WA 2017.37. Image © Ashmolean Museum, University of Oxford.

to indicate the shape of the eye and the curling moustache have been completely worn away from the surface, the only surviving traces being the ends of the threads as the stitches disappear through the remains of the satin.

Agents of decay

Conservators refer to the various factors that cause damage to historic material as 'agents of decay'. Seven agents can be identified as contributing to the damaged condition of surviving seventeenth-century needlework in the Ashmolean collection. These agents have interacted and worked together, resulting in the current condition of the embroideries. It is the role of conservators to carry out conservation measures, both preventive and interventive, which will keep the impact of the agents of decay to a minimum while the objects are under their care.

1. Light

One of the most obvious ways embroideries change over time is the fading of the colours originally used in the designs. This can be seen dramatically when images of the front and back of an embroidery are viewed side by side. Fig. 4.3a shows a detail of the reverse of a panel depicting an Old Testament scene. Here the pink,

Fig. 4.3a
Old Testament scene, detail of reverse, 1650–1700. WA 2009.168.2. Image © Ashmolean Museum, University of Oxford.

Fig. 4.3b
Old Testament scene, detail of front, 1650–1700. WA 2009.168.2. Image © Ashmolean Museum, University of Oxford.

red and yellow silk threads have not been exposed to light, and the original vivid colours remain. In contrast, the front of the same area of the embroidery has lost almost all its colour due to light damage (Fig. 4.3b), leaving only a pale shadow of the worker's original vision. Visible light is the radiation in the electromagnetic spectrum to which the human eye is sensitive, typically wavelengths ranging from 400 to 700 nanometres (nm). Exposure to this type of radiation is what primarily causes light-sensitive colour pigments to fade and this is why embroideries in museums are displayed under low visible light levels. In addition to causing colours to fade, exposure to other types of radiation will also result in fibres becoming weak and brittle. Common light sources (including the sun) emit shorter wavelength, non-visible, ultraviolet (UV) radiation. UV radiation has wavelengths shorter than 400nm. The energy in this type of radiation mainly causes the weakening and yellowing of textile fibres. UV radiation can be removed from visible light with filters.[5]

2. Insect damage

The larval stages of certain species of insects feed on proteinaceous materials such as hair and feathers often found as decorative elements in seventeenth-century needlework. Evidence of insect damage can be seen in several of the embroideries in the Ashmolean. Fig. 4.4a shows a detail from the panel *Solomon and the Queen of Sheba*. The hairstyle of the Queen's maid has been created from bundles of light-coloured hair stitched down with silk thread over a base of silk wrapped coils of

Fig. 4.4a
Picture panel, *Solomon and the Queen of Sheba*, detail of the Queen's maid, 1650–1700. WA 1994.142. Image © Ashmolean Museum, University of Oxford.

Fig. 4.4b
Picture panel, *Solomon and the Queen of Sheba*, detail of the hair of the Queen's maid with insect damage, 1650–1700. WA 1994.142, Image © Ashmolean Museum, University of Oxford.

wire. Under higher magnification (Fig. 4.4b) it is evident that areas of the hair have been consumed and grazed. Where embroiderers have used feathers they have been similarly attacked. This type of damage is typical of the larvae of the varied carpet beetle (*anthrenus verbasci*). Other pests found in Britain that frequently cause damage to hair, feathers and woollen textiles are the webbing clothes moth (*tineola bisselliella*) and case-bearing clothes moth (*tinea pellionella*).

3. Inherent vice: physical

Physical inherent vice can be defined as the potential for damage created by the way in which an object is constructed. In seventeenth-century needlework this can relate to the vulnerability of decorative applied elements such as spangles or pearls, or the way the embroideries have been mounted or framed. The beads, mica, pearls and other three-dimensional elements are vulnerable to loss and damage because, by their raised nature, they are in the locations most likely to be touched or brushed against during use. In addition, as they age, the fibres of the threads which sew the decorative elements onto the embroidery are weakened and tend to break, leading to losses. This can be seen in a mica window applied to the Old Testament scene referred to above (Fig. 4.5), now precariously held in place by a single stitch, others being broken, damaged or entirely lost. Construction processes can also introduce physical tensions into an embroidery. The traditional technique of mounting needlework on a board with lacing across the back keeps the textile permanently taut, but as materials age and weaken such tension will eventually result in physical damage. This can be seen at the edge of one of the

Fig. 4.5
Old Testament scene, detail of front with degraded stitching around mica window, 1650–1700. WA 2009.168.1. Image © Ashmolean Museum, University of Oxford.

Fig. 4.6
Picture panel *The Four Continents,* detail of top edge with splits in satin ground fabric, mid to late seventeenth century, Feller collection, WA 2014.71.55. Image © Ashmolean Museum, University of Oxford.

framed panels in the Ashmolean, *The Four Continents* (Fig. 4.6). Large stitches can be seen tensioning the embroidery around a backboard; the satin on the edge of the panel has developed splits as the fibres have weakened with age.

4. Inherent vice: chemical

Whereas physical inherent vice refers to the way an object has been constructed, chemical inherent vice refers to the chemical composition of the components of an object. This type of degradation is the reason why so many of the black threads used in seventeenth-century embroideries have been lost. The tannin dyes and iron sulphate mordants used to dye the black threads mean these fibres have gone through a very acid process, and the sulphate ions from the mordant form sulphuric acid in humid conditions, causing the decomposition of the fibres.[6] A detail from *The Proclamation of Solomon* (Fig. 4.7a) illustrates the fragility of the degraded fibres. Under higher magnification the black threads of the maid's headdress can be seen to be falling into tiny fragments (Fig. 4.7b). This is another instance where standard conservation techniques for surface cleaning the object would result in substantial losses. Any attempt at lifting off surface soiling with low-power vacuum suction would also remove quantities of the black embroidery thread.

5. Environment

The fifth agent of decay is the quality of the environment in which the embroidery exists. This could be affected by levels of air pollution, humidity, temperature and the type of box, drawer or frame in which the textile was kept. The sulphur content and soot particles common in the polluted air of British towns during the

Fig. 4.7a
Picture panel, *The Proclamation of Solomon*, detail of the maid's headdress, mid to late seventeenth century, WA 1947.191.313. Image © Ashmolean Museum, University of Oxford.

Fig. 4.7b
Picture panel, *The Proclamation of Solomon*, detail of the maid's headdress under higher magnification, mid to late seventeenth century, WA 1947.191.313. Image © Ashmolean Museum, University of Oxford.

eighteenth, nineteenth and early twentieth centuries were very harmful to embroideries. Soot particles deposited directly onto textiles created layers of soiling. The sulphur content of polluted air formed acidic compounds which, in the presence of moisture and heat, reacted with silk and metal threads, resulting in the discoloration and weakening of the silk and the tarnishing of the metal threads.[7] Wooden backboards and frames can be another source of acidity that contributes to the deterioration of embroideries. When wooden elements form part of the original construction of an object, as in a casket, it is important to consider what elements of the environment can be controlled without compromising the true nature of the complete object. A stable, non-fluctuating environment, free from additional sources of pollutants is usually the most appropriate option for these objects.

6. People: pre-museum damage

The final two agents of decay refer to the actions of people, both before and after a textile has become part of a museum collection. An embroidered bodice in the Ashmolean (Fig. 4.8a) illustrates the way people can act as an agent of decay. The bodice lining has been rubbed into holes (Fig. 4.8b) while the garment was worn before it became part of a museum collection. The choices people have made in mounting and framing embroideries can be another cause of decay. If the materials used are not conservation grade they can be a source of acidity, which will cause textile fibres to decay and weaken.

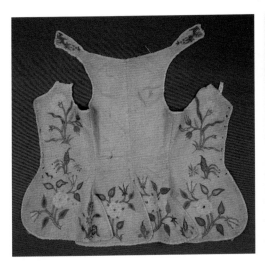

Fig. 4.8a
Embroidered bodice, seventeenth century, WA 1990.45. Image © Ashmolean Museum, University of Oxford.

Fig. 4.8b
Embroidered bodice, wear to lining, seventeenth century. WA 1990.45. Image © Ashmolean Museum, University of Oxford.

7. People: museum damage

Once a textile has entered a museum collection it is still subject to agents of decay. Even careful handling during teaching and exhibition preparation can lead to damage. The role of conservation is to slow down decay.

Conservation strategies

In order to keep damage caused by the agents of decay to a minimum, a range of techniques is used to ensure the embroideries are cared for in the best possible fashion. Preventive conservation measures include: ensuring environmental conditions are appropriate; making improvements to storage, handling and display systems; and, carrying out integrated pest management (IPM), which prevents damaging insect infestations in the collection.

Interventive conservation measures are carried out on individual embroideries and include cleaning and conservation support treatments to improve the appearance of textiles and ensure they are stable in preparation for display and study.

A successful preventive conservation measure is one that enables an object to fulfil its roles with minimal effect on its condition while maximising its accessibility for study and display. The *Frog Purse* is a very popular piece, required for display in the Textile Gallery as well as being regularly requested for viewing by scholars and special interest groups. In collaboration with the museum mount-maker, a mount has been developed (Fig. 4.9) that allows these various needs to be met with minimal handling. The purse lies on an acrylic tray, which can be secured in the

Fig. 4.9
Frog purse, on acrylic mount, seventeenth century, WA 1947.191.324. Image © Ashmolean Museum, University of Oxford.

drawer but still easily lifted out using two discreet handles. Six curved acrylic pegs hold the frog in place on the tray while also allowing it to be gently lifted off so its spotted tummy can be viewed and then easily returned to the mount.

Interventive conservation treatments on the embroideries can involve gentle surface cleaning, although as was noted earlier, this is always done using a microscope so that only soiling is removed and not delicate or loosely attached parts of the embroidery. Other interventive treatments could include: the replacement of old acidic backboards with a conservation grade, acid-free alternative; minimising areas of loss with colour-matched patches; and, stabilising or attaching loose or vulnerable elements more securely.

However, time cannot be turned back and interventive conservation measures do not provide a magic wand that can return an object to its original appearance. Instead, the emphasis must be on preventing any further damage by understanding the agents of decay which act upon this type of embroidery and promoting preventive measures such as safe storage and careful handling. If these are successful, it means that despite his fragile condition, a seventeenth-century embroidered gentleman, such as the one depicted on the Kiel casket (Fig. 4.2a), can continue to fulfil a role of enabling people to learn about these fascinating English embroideries and the period in which they were made.

Notes

[1] See Catalogue, pp. 106-107.

[2] *The Sacrifice of Isaac,* Ashmolean Museum WA OA.414; documented in Sonia O'Connor and Mary M. Brooks, ' "In needle works these doth great knowledge rest": The contribution of X-radiography to the understanding of seventeenth-century English embroiseries from the Ashmolean Museums of Art and Archaeology, Oxford', in *X-radiography of Textiles, Dress and Related Objects,* edited by Sonia O'Connor and Mary M. Brooks (Oxford: Butterworth-Heinemann, 2007), pp. 237-248, at pp. 238-240.

[3] *Solomon and the Queen of Sheba,* Ashmolean Museum WA 1994.142.

[4] For example, *The Sacrifice of Isaac;* O'Connor and Brooks, op. cit., pp. 238-240.

[5] Stefan Michalski, *Agent of Deterioration: Light, Ultraviolet and Infrared* (Canadian Conservation Institute, 2017). https://www.canada.ca/en/conservation-institute/services/agents-deterioration/light.html [accessed 25 April 2018].

[6] Ágnes Tímár-Balázsy and Dinah Eastop, *Chemical Principles of Textile Conservation* (Oxford: Butterworth-Heinemann, 1998), pp. 95-96.

[7] Ibid., pp. 47 and 135-137.

5 The pencil's excellency: Designing a contemporary casket in the seventeenth-century style

Nicola Jarvis

Drawing from seventeenth-century raised work

The curious aesthetics of seventeenth-century English raised embroidery captured my imagination almost two decades ago when the re-creation of Elizabethan- and Stuart-style textiles was becoming popular again in the embroidery world. I needed to find out more about this particular style and visited textile collections in museums, historic houses and other venues in England and North America in order to make drawings and to photograph raised-work stitching. A deep love of nature coupled with an enjoyment in drawing plants, birds and insects drove my fascination for this unique historic embroidery. As a designer, I was particularly interested in how the natural forms were stylised and interpreted in the patterns and stitches of the period.

After studying numerous embroidered picture panels, caskets and mirror frames, I re-created this distinctive imagery through detailed drawings, and replicated various raised elements such as animals, birds and fish worked in needle lace slips in order to understand how they had been made. I used the action of intricate drawing to explore how elements like three-dimensional trees, fruits and flowers were constructed in a variety of padded and wired techniques (Fig. 5.1).

These preliminary investigations led to the creation of a three-dimensional drawing of a casket and my first major art-making response to seventeenth-century raised embroidery (Fig. 5.2). This elaborate box was made for a fellow embroiderer to commemorate his fortieth birthday in 2010, and appropriated the typical style and arrangement of motifs found on extant casket lids and picture panels. I framed a portrait of my colleague in an ornate cartouche surrounded by a profusion of plants and insects, in the style of a lavish casket panel dating from the third quarter of the seventeenth century, now in the Metropolitan Museum of Art, New York (Fig. 5.3a

Fig. 5.1
Nicola Jarvis,
Raised work
strawberry,
colour pencil
on board, 2010.
© Nicola Jarvis.

& b).[1] On this historic piece, the figure of the Roman goddess Flora – said to be a
portrait of Elizabeth Coombe, 'the most celebrated needlewoman of her period'[2] –
is depicted in seventeenth-century English dress.

The 'Flora' panel is typical of raised work pictures made during the Interregnum
and Restoration periods. The particular style of this piece has been attributed to
the workshop of the pattern drawer and embroiderer John Nelham. Panels thought
to be by him often have a central cartouche decorated with a vellum fringe
adorned with scrolling leaves worked in loops of silk-wrapped purl threads and
cornflowers placed at intervals around the frame. Animals rest on hillocks, insects

Fig. 5.2
Nicola Jarvis,
Seventeenth-
century style
casket, colour
pencil on board,
2010. © Nicola
Jarvis

Fig. 5.3a
Nicola Jarvis, Seventeenth-
century style casket, detail on
lid, colour pencil on board, 2010.
© Nicola Jarvis.

Fig. 5.3b
Casket panel featuring a Lady, said to be Elizabeth
Coombe, detail, third quarter of the seventeenth century,
Metropolitan Museum of Art 64.101.1326. © Metropolitan
Museum of Art, New York.

flutter around a pale silk satin ground dotted with silver gilt spangles and flower
slips ornament the four corners of the picture plane.

John Nelham lived and worked in London, where he inherited his father Roger's
embroidery business in 1653. The Nelhams' working practice was very similar to
mine today, and like me, they had a library of visual material, embroidery frames
and equipment, which would certainly have comprised measuring tapes or rules,
writing and drawing implements, needles, pins, scissors and tweezers. Textile
historian John Nevinson discovered the will of Roger Nelham, made in 1653, in
which he bequeathed to John, 'the halfe of my books and prints and patterns,
which I do use for the drawings of workes... all my beames and lathes and working
instruments... which do appertain and belong to my worke house.'[3] It is both
fascinating and comforting that little has changed between a hand embroiderer's
work almost four hundred years ago and his modern counterpart.

The Nelhams' method of transferring designs has changed very little since the
seventeenth century. Light from a window, or a candle positioned underneath the
embroidery frame was used as an early form of light box to trace the motifs onto
the mounted fabric (Fig. 5.4). Pattern drawers also employed the ancient process of
prick and pounce where the design is marked out on paper by puncturing tiny holes
along the design lines and rubbing charcoal or chalk powder through the holes onto
the fabric. Once the paper is removed, the fine dots of charcoal or chalk are traced
over with a tiny brush and paint, or pen and ink. I still use this process today when I
need to transfer a design onto a thick or dark fabric where the light will not pass
through the surface easily.

Fig. 5.4
Alessandro
Paganino, *Libro
primo. De
rechami per
elquale se
impara in diuersi
modi lordine e il
modo de
recamare: cosa
non mai piu
fatta ne stata
mostrata, et qual
modo se insegna
al lettore
voltando la carta*
(Venice, 1527),
facsimile reprint
(Venice: F.
Ongania, 1878).
Photo Nicola
Jarvis, Courtesy
of the Victoria
and Albert
Museum,
London.

A seventeenth-century casket project produced by a designer-embroiderer like John
Nelham would have comprised a set of panel designs, or pattern pieces, hand-drawn
or painted onto silk satin or linen (Fig. 5.5), together with a range of coloured silks and
metal threads for working the embroidery. In some cases, selected areas may have
been started by the designer to demonstrate suitable stitch techniques. It was also
common for private tutors or teachers in girls' boarding schools to guide their young
students in working the designs as part of their education. In addition to designing
needlework patterns, professional embroiderers and their assistants would have been
commissioned to work whole panels and caskets for their customers.

Fig. 5.5
Unfinished
cabinet panels,
c. 1660,
Metropolitan
Museum of Art
1998.541. ©
Metropolitan
Museum of Art,
New York.

In my practice, I design, produce and supply a range of custom-made projects and embroidery kits to a wide community of stitchers. *Ornamental Embroidery's Oak Tree* casket project is a perfect example of the same bespoke, seventeenth-century "kit" service being continued today (Fig. 5.6).

Designing a twenty-first century raised work casket

My role as designer and technical advisor for the *Oak Tree* casket project was key in realising and composing the numerous motifs for each of the panels. Whilst working on the designs and researching the historic objects and craftspeople employed in this industry, I have found many similarities between my practice and that of designer-embroiderers like John Nelham. I also align myself with artists like Jacques Le Moyne de Morgues (c. 1533–1588), a Huguenot cartographer, draughtsman and painter who made accurate illustrations of plant forms through the use of pen and ink, printmaking, brush and pigment.[4] His drive and ability to render subject matter from life was akin to my own art-making practice, where I place great value in drawing and painting botanical subject matter from life, where possible. Le Moyne de Morgues published a collection of botanical illustrations in a pattern book entitled *Le Clef des Champs* (1586), in which each plant is faithfully depicted and labelled with its Latin, French and English names (Fig. 5.7).

Fig. 5.6
Contemporary casket panel designed by Nicola Jarvis and partially stitched by Clare Lobb.
© Photo Nicola Jarvis.

Other notable artists and publishers producing botanical and natural history pattern books during this period include John Gerarde, Crispijn van de Passe II and Peter Stent, but in contrast to Le Moyne de Morgues, who demonstrated rigour and authenticity in generating original artwork for his publication, many of their images were appropriated and reproduced from earlier manuscripts and printed texts. Nevertheless, this wealth of available imagery became an invaluable resource for designer-embroiderers like Nelham to use in their commissioned work (Fig. 5.8).

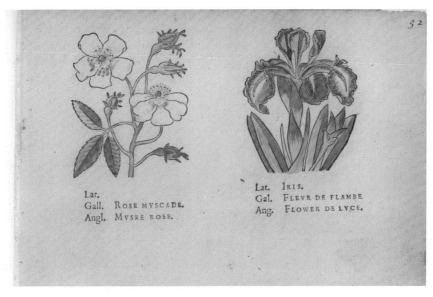

Fig. 5.7
Musk rose and iris from Jacques Le Moyne de Morgues, *La Clef des Champs* (1586). © The Trustees of the British Museum.

Fig. 5.8
Linen canvas
with animal
motifs, pen and
ink drawing,
1600–1625,
Victoria and
Albert Museum
T.88-1925.
© Victoria and
Albert Museum,
London.

Fig. 5.9
Pet cats copied
from images
taken on a
mobile phone,
transferred in
ink and hand-
coloured on silk
satin ready for
stitching,
designed by
Nicola Jarvis,
2013. © Nicola
Jarvis.

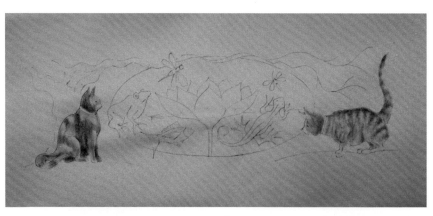

Fig. 5.10
Traditional stag
and leopard
motifs designed
by Nicola Jarvis
and stitched by
Dorie Clark.
© Photo Nicola
Jarvis.

Fig. 5.11a & b
Nicola Jarvis,
Design
proposal and
worked model
for the two-day
Oak Tree panel
raised work
course, 2012.
© Nicola Jarvis.

Whilst Nelham and his contemporaries resorted to engravings and woodcuts of botanical, zoological or decorative motifs to create their patterns, for the *Oak Tree* casket designs I copied photographs of subject matter the students wanted to have featured on their panels (Fig. 5.9). The technology of photography for recording nature and life events has become a major resource for today's designer. Internet search engines have replaced printed encyclopaedias and reference books, and now virtual inspiration boards like Pinterest, Google images and similar online picture stocks have become today's pattern books. However, some of the students specifically wanted to use a selection of seventeenth-century designs, so I appropriated elements directly from historic pieces and re-created simplified patterns for them to stitch their new interpretations (Fig. 5.10).

The casket project evolved from a two-day raised work course held at the Ashmolean Museum in 2012 called the *Oak Tree* panel, which introduced the fundamentals of padded, wrapped and wired stitch techniques. *The Sacrifice of Isaac* (1673), an elaborate raised work picture in the Museum's textile collection, was the main inspiration for the design of this contemporary panel, and was used to re-create the composition and elements typical of the period style (see Fig. 1.1a). However, instead of a religious or Classical scene, I chose to depict a universal subject in the central cartouche, preferring to celebrate natural history by paying homage to the 350-year-old oak tree in my Warwickshire garden (Fig. 5.11a & b). In using this motif I was also referencing the legend of the Royal Oak at Boscobel in Worcestershire in which Charles II is thought to have hidden from the Parliamentarians in 1651.

The students enjoyed the short *Oak Tree* course and were eager to progress their skills and develop the initial panel into a seventeenth-century style casket. Once we negotiated, timetabled and planned the four-year course, the *Oak Tree* casket maquette was developed as a feasibility study to investigate the possibilities and limitations of the design and construction of a contemporary box (Fig. 5.12).

Fig. 5.12
Nicola Jarvis,
Oak Tree casket
maquette,
colour pencil on
board, 2012.
© Nicola Jarvis.

Fig. 5.13a
Marigold pricked and pounced from Richard Shoreleyker, *A Schole-house for the Needle* (1632), facsimile edition (Much Wenlock: RJL Smith & Associates, 1998). Photo Lynn Hulse, Courtesy of Elizabeth Mason and RJL Smith & Associates.

Fig. 5.13b
Marigold from the picture panel *The Sacrifice of Isaac,* 1673, Ashmolean Museum WA OA.414. Image reproduced with kind permission of Ashmolean Museum, University of Oxford.

Fig. 5.13c & d
Design from the *Oak Tree* panel, colour pencil on board, and embroidered marigold from casket lid, stitched by Nicola Jarvis, 2012. © Nicola Jarvis.

Including the lid, each casket comprised nine panels, with four lid friezes, two short sides and two long sides. With twenty-two students joining the course, I designed and hand-draughted 176 individual compositions. Adopting the same workshop practices as the Nelhams, I employed both the lightbox and the prick and pounce method to transfer the motifs to the silk satin ground. In one copy of Richard Shorleyker's 1632 pattern book A *Schole-house for the Needle* there is a page that has been used to prick and pounce a marigold motif where the pricked holes and haze of rubbed charcoal are still evident (Fig. 5.13a). The marigold is very similar to one that I appropriated from *The Sacrifice of Isaac* panel (Fig. 5.13b) in composing the lid design. The antique and modern examples (Fig. 5.13c & d) of this floral motif make for an interesting comparison.

Creating compositions for each panel from the numerous requested motifs and images supplied was an extensive activity, enjoyable and challenging in equal measure. Yet, the most rewarding aspect of the project was participating in the transformation of the line designs into stitched works. These seemed to take on a life and momentum all of their own. For a designer, it is particularly gratifying to experience students interpreting initial ideas through a myriad of colours, shapes and textures, especially when they begin to manage their own decisions and produce work that looks even more effective than initially envisaged.

We have no evidence as to whether the Nelhams would have seen their designed works executed and finished by their customers. However, I feel privileged to have played a part in the making of the contemporary casket panels beyond my involvement in the design process. Having a record of the development of the caskets, from initial concepts through to the finished objects, has produced a rich document of the learning process that benefitted greatly from looking at extant historic objects to gain ideas and compare working methods and techniques.

In the original plan, the intention was for the students to hand stitch the embroidered panels together to form the final casket construction. After much consideration, I felt that the mounted raised work panels would look more professional and authentic displayed on an actual wooden box. The Education Department at the Ashmolean contacted the in-house cabinetmakers and it was agreed that a master cabinetmaker would construct bespoke caskets with recessed panels on all sides made from a variety of woods, including cherry, walnut and mahogany, in which to house the finished and mounted embroidered works. This decision enabled the students to create a collection of objects that combined historic style and technique with contemporary imagery and handling. The caskets made fascinating viewing when displayed in the Museum setting alongside original seventeenth-century embroideries during *The Needles Excellency* exhibition in 2017.

When I think about all the panels and caskets that I have looked at or been involved in making, they strike me as a mesmerising celebration of life stories, each vignette interwoven with a love of the natural world and a delight in hand-making. The opportunity for interpreting personal narrative and symbolism for the students' casket panels created a profound opportunity for heirlooms to be made as important and beautiful records of family and social history. During the period of designing and developing the caskets it became apparent to me that the intention of both the modern stitcher and her seventeenth-century counterpart was to assemble and create a collection of imagery that held particular significance in her life. These contemporary caskets were made to be passed down to future generations as a souvenir of love and remembrance of family occasions and personal histories.

Notes

[1] Andrew Morrall and Melinda Watt, eds, *English Embroidery form The Metropolitan Museum of Art, 1580-1700. 'Twixt Art and Nature* (New Haven/London, Yale University Press, Bard Graduate Center & Metropolitan Museum of Art, 2008), pp. 222-223; Margaret Swain, 'John Nelham's Needlework Panel', *The Bulletin of the Needle and Bobbin Club,* vol. 65, nos 1-2, (1982), pp. 3-16.

[2] Morrall and Watt, op. cit., p. 222.

[3] John L. Nevinson, 'John Nelham, Embroiderer', *The Bulletin of the Needle and Bobbin Club,* vol. 65, nos 1-2 (1982), pp. 17-19, at p. 17.

[4] Paul Hulton, ed., *The work of Jacques Le Moyne de Morgues: A Huguenot artist in France, Florida and England,* 2 vols (London: British Museum Press, 1977).

CATALOGUE OF CONTEMPORARY
RAISED EMBROIDERY

1   Nicola Jarvis

The design for the casket lid, which unites many of the boxes on display, was adapted from the 1673 panel *The Sacrifice of Isaac*, bequeathed to the Ashmolean Museum in 1947 by the noted connoisseur John Francis Mallett, Chairman of Mallett Antiques. The single floral motifs dominating the four corners of the original panel – common to a number of embroideries dating from the Stuart period – have been retained. In place of the Old Testament narrative featured in the original central cartouche I have chosen to depict an oak tree festooned with three-dimensional leaves and acorns, inspired by the 350-year-old oak in my Warwickshire garden. The remaining ground is covered with winged insects and a snail inspired by seventeenth-century pattern books.

Fig. 1.1
Casket designed and stitched by Nicola Jarvis.
© Photo David Gowers.

Fig. 1.2
Maquette
designed by
Nicola Jarvis,
colour pencil on
board, 2012.
© Photo David
Gowers.

Fig. 1.3
Maquette lid and
frieze, designed by
Nicola Jarvis,
colour pencil on
board, 2012.
© Nicola Jarvis.

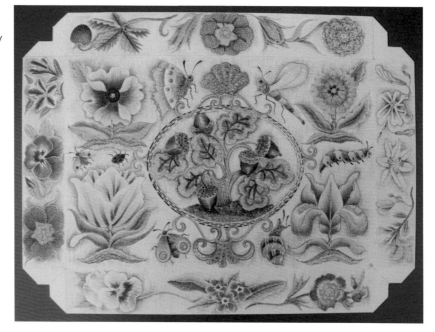

2 Jane Bawn

I have long held a fascination with seventeenth-century embroidery, particularly raised work in all its forms, and although this project has been a steep learning curve for me, I have really enjoyed the journey.

The motifs for the frieze were inspired by my Dad, who enjoyed pottering in his greenhouse, tending his grapevine, and my grandmother, who always had pansies growing under her windowsill.

Water has been a major factor in my life as our family business is in water treatment, and having obtained a Royal Warrant for services to Her Majesty the Queen in 2009, the water feature on the front panel had to take centre stage.

I live near the home of the Royal Navy at Portsmouth, where Henry VIII's warship *The Mary Rose* is on display. The vessel is represented on a side panel by a Tudor rose, one of my favourite images from the period. (I have ideas for taking this theme further into a larger cabinet.) The birds, small animals and flora were chosen because of my love of nature. The trees and mounds on the back panel are like a sampler of the different types of plant found on the original cabinets.

Fig. 2.1
Casket designed by Nicola Jarvis and stitched by Jane Bawn.
© Photo David Gowers.

Fig. 2.2
Front and back
panels with water
feature and trees,
work in progress.
© Photo David
Gowers.

Fig. 2.3
Side panel with
Tudor rose motif
before mounting.
© Photo Lynn
Hulse.

3 Susanna Blackshaw

The lid shows a classic boat, the Bristol Channel Pilot Cutter Alpha. The Pilot Cutter owners were privateers, and their boats sat out in the Western Approaches of the Atlantic, looking for incoming sailing ships. The first to deliver their pilot onto the incoming vessel won the job of navigating it through the difficult waters of the Bristol Channel. Alpha appeared on the scene in 1904. She became renowned for her speed and sea kindliness, and there was substantial interest in her provenance and in the shape of her hull. Unlike most of the Bristol Channel Cutters, Alpha was built in Fleetwood.

When the days of sailing pilots ended in 1924, the cutters were subsequently much sought after as private yachts. Alpha was sold by the Prosser family into private hands. In 1989 she was purchased and restored by Michael Humphries and run as a sailing tour ship in the Hebrides. The constellation illustrated is Bootes.

The side panels display two invertebrate species whose giant nerve cells made feasible experimental work on ion channels in nerve cell membranes. The sea slug *Archidoris pseudoargus* is a marine gastropod, and the medicinal leech *Hirudo medicinalis* is a fresh-water annelid.

Fig. 3.1
Casket designed by Nicola Jarvis and stitched by Susanna Blackshaw. © Photo David Gowers.

Fig. 3.2
Work in progress on the side panels. © Photo Lynn Hulse.

4   Gill Brunning

I enjoyed this project. I always do enjoy the act of stitching, sitting needle in hand, transforming the blank space into a multi-coloured picture, appearing to be deedily occupied while really doing nothing at all. 'What's not to like?'

But asking me 'What inspired these images?' leaves me at a loss. They form no part of the history of my life; they tell no story, they are just pictures, half memories of other pictures, which vary from Winnie the Pooh to the Dutch art viewed in museums.

I had fun making them – thank you for tutoring me.

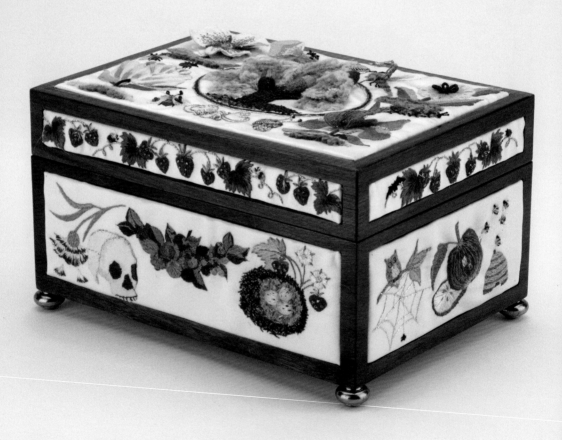

Fig. 4.1
Casket designed by Nicola Jarvis and stitched by Gill Brunning.
© Photo David Gowers.

Fig. 4.2
Front and back panels before mounting.
© Photo David Gowers.

5 Kate Busby

My life in stitches

From a very young age I embroidered and stitched with my Granny and Mum, but it wasn't until 2003, when visiting a local exhibition, that I became aware of the existence of raised work. I was so fascinated by it that I wanted to "have a go".

While attending classes at the Royal School of Needlework I found out about the *Oak Tree* casket course at the Ashmolean Museum. I joined the *Ornamental Embroidery* group and a whole new world began to open up to me. We were given the design for the lid top but were allowed to decide what images we each wanted on the remaining panels of the lid and box. After some thought, I settled on the theme of 'my life in stitches'. Inspiration came from growing up on my family's farm near Market Bosworth, Leicestershire in the 1960s and 1970s, surrounded by animals and nature. I had always been very aware of the Battle of Bosworth and the War of the Roses, so after recent events involving the discovery of Richard III's body, I decided one panel should be dedicated to this theme. Each of the images has a special meaning for me, reflecting memories or events in my life.

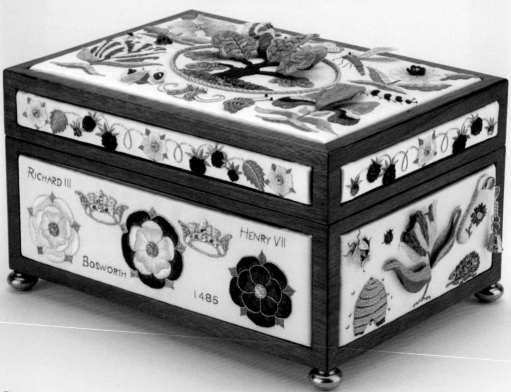

Fig. 5.1
Casket designed by Nicola Jarvis and stitched by Kate Busby.
© Photo David Gowers.

Fig. 5.2
Side panel before mounting.
© Photo David Gowers.

Fig. 5.3
Side panel and frieze before mounting.
© Photo David Gowers.

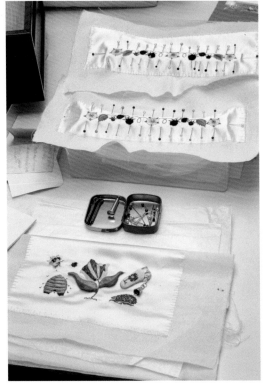

6 Aileen Cahill

Now and then: my life in stitches

Endless hours by the sea, fishing, swimming and playing with Simba our family dog; the great blue whale on the family crest, my Dad said was our eternal quarry. Home was wrapped in Virginia creeper; Irish country hedgerows full of the scents of fuchsia and honeysuckle; Michael's vine growing over our pond in London. Eventually we will have that vintage pinot noir. The pond itself a great draw for wildlife and for Honey and Archie, our curious cats.

Fig. 6.1
Casket designed by Nicola Jarvis and stitched by Aileen Cahill.
© Photo David Gowers.

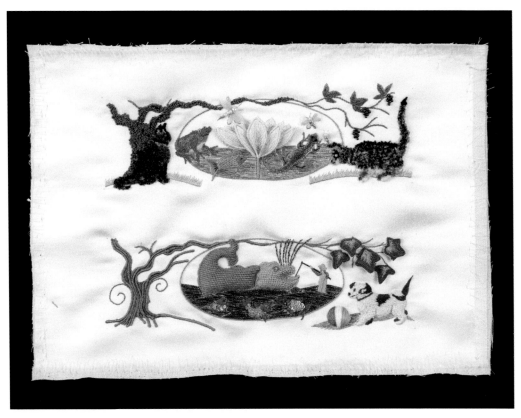

Fig. 6.2
Front and back panels before mounting.
© Photo David Gowers.

7   Marilyn Chalke

I loved every moment of this project. It started in 2012 as a two-day course stitching a panel. It was such an exciting piece of work that it quickly turned into a project, thanks to Nicola Jarvis and Lynn Hulse.

Having completed what became the lid of the casket, we then had to think of a design for the frieze and side panels. Initially this was a challenge, but as I love flowers, it became clear that flora would be my theme. A love of flowers started during my childhood, with both parents being very keen gardeners.

I thought about the language of flowers, their meanings and significance, and found books relating to this very helpful. As an example, Daisy means cheerfulness/sentiment, Honeysuckle, devotion and Lily of the Valley, return of happiness.

I wanted to use my favourite stitch techniques of gold and silk work for this project. My threads of choice were Soie d'Alger and Mulberry silks. The gold used included pearl purl, spangles, bright check and smooth purl. The stitches included needle lace, long and short, satin stitch and laid work.

Fig. 7.1
Casket designed by Nicola Jarvis and stitched
by Marilyn Chalke. © Photo David Gowers.

We were privileged to be offered wooden caskets made by the cabinetmaker at the Ashmolean Museum. From a selection of woods on offer, American dark cherry complemented the colours in my embroidered panels and so became my wood of choice.

Sadly the course came to an end, but I have learnt so much in the process with huge thanks to Nicola and Lynn, and I have a piece of work with many fond memories.

Fig. 7.2
Side panel before mounting.
© Photo David Gowers.

Fig. 7.3
Front and back panels before mounting.
© Photo David Gowers.

8   Dorie Clark

For the four side panels of my casket I chose subjects that were meaningful to me in different ways. My interest in raised work embroidery goes back quite a few years now and so the two side panels depicting the heraldic animals (stag, lion, unicorn and leopard) were chosen because they were popular subjects in early raised work pieces and use stitches and techniques found in historic examples. I chose the mermaid's grotto (again a popular historic setting) because it was fun, slightly risqué, and I loved the iridescent sequins. On a more personal note, the panel of the house flanked by fruit trees is of our home in Canterbury for forty years. The fruit trees no longer inhabit the garden but they are a reminder of the many happy years we have spent there.

Fig. 8.1
Casket designed by Nicola Jarvis and stitched
by Dorie Clark. © Photo David Gowers.

Fig. 8.2
Lion and unicorn side panel before
mounting. © Photo Lynn Hulse.

Fig. 8.3
Long panel depicting an Edwardian
home in Kent before mounting.
© Photo Nicola Jarvis.

Fig. 8.4
Gluing the stag and leopard side panel into the
recess on the wooden box. © Photo Lynn Hulse.

9 Sandra Deacon

The inspiration for my casket was the historic raised work pieces in the Ashmolean Museum. I love to do traditional stitchery and saw this as an opportunity to follow in the footsteps of the seventeenth-century ladies and girls who created this lovely work.

The embroidery was stitched on a silk satin fabric, mainly in stranded silk thread but with small amounts of cotton perle for the French knots. Padding was done with layers of felt for the castle, which was then stitched in long and short stitch, and with soft string for the fountains and insects. All the wired elements were stitched onto silk organza or worked in needle lace.

Fig. 9.1
Casket designed by Nicola Jarvis and stitched by Sandra Deacon. © Photo Sandra Deacon.

Fig. 9.2
Long panel designed by Nicola Jarvis and stitched by Sandra Deacon. © Photo Sandra Deacon.

Fig. 9.3
Long panel designed by Nicola Jarvis and stitched by Sandra Deacon. © Photo Sandra Deacon.

Fig. 9.4
Side panel designed by Nicola Jarvis and stitched by Sandra Deacon. © Photo Lynn Hulse.

10 Sue Fowler

My casket is a reflection of family, flora and inspiration.

I chose the Welsh dragon, the leek and the daffodil to represent my Dad and his heritage, a down-to-earth man. The other side panel depicts the Northamptonshire rose and trees for my Mum, a graceful woman. I chose the architectural feature because it reminds me of happy times spent at Hampton Court with the Royal School of Needlework, a wonderful experience. The use of flowers and bugs reflect my love of gardening; however, I'm afraid stitching wins hands down for my time!

Creating this piece of embroidery has been a rewarding experience. Working with different threads and techniques certainly took me out of my comfort zone. Part of the experience and equally important, were meeting new people and learning together.

Fig. 10.1
Welsh panel designed by Nicola Jarvis and stitched by Sue Fowler. © Photo Sue Fowler.

Fig. 10.2
Northamptonshire panel designed by Nicola Jarvis and stitched by Sue Fowler. © Photo Sue Fowler.

Fig. 10.3
Architectural panel designed by Nicola Jarvis and stitched by Sue Fowler. © Photo Sue Fowler.

11 Sally Giffen

I enjoy examining seventeenth-century raised work embroidery, in particular the flora and fauna displayed in this work. Embroiderers in the past have stitched grinning lions, proud peacocks, aerodynamically unsound bees and butterflies, and fish almost begging to be caught. The stitchers have, I hope, had as much pleasure in their creations as I get from looking at them.

My casket is based on the idea of the four elements – Air, Earth, Fire and Water – and the creatures that inhabit them, as well as a grey tabby modelled on my own cat, which supervises me while I am working.

The front and back panels represent 'Air' (bird, bee, butterfly, ladybird, plus cat) and 'Earth' (lion, peacock, rabbit, plus cat) respectively. The side panels comprise 'Fire' (phoenix rising from the flames, salamander, plus cat) and 'Water' (golden fish, frog, plus cat).

It was a pleasure and a privilege to work with Lynn Hulse and Nicola Jarvis who, had the unenviable task of sketching the designs based on the stitcher's ideas, as well as Jude Barrett from the Ashmolean Education Department and the cabinetmaker Paul Evett, who made up the box on which the work is mounted.

Fig. 11.1
Casket designed by Nicola Jarvis and stitched by Sally Giffen.
© Photo David Gowers.

Fig. 11.2
Side panel 'Fire'.
© Photo David Gowers.

Fig. 11.3
Side panel 'Water'.
© Photo David Gowers.

Fig. 11.4
Mounting the frieze panels.
© Photo Lynn Hulse.

12 Karen Goldie-Morrison

A secret garden

A butterfly net among wildflowers on a sunny country day is amongst my earliest memories. A childhood passion for collecting insects matured into my love of natural history. An early stint in wildlife publishing led to my joining a wildlife film company whose cameramen captured the private lives of animals and plants in groundbreaking detail and in truly memorable images.

Playing with embroidery stitches and fabric was another outlet for my fascination with colour and structure. After a lifetime of stitching, I now focus my efforts on embroidery projects, like the casket, which are several years in the making.

As a child, I would lie down in the grass to appreciate an insect-eye view of the world. My casket invokes this close-up on nature. The side panels display a flower meadow, spangled with wild plants, a holly blue butterfly flitting past and noisy with bees buzzing. The garden gate in the front panel opens to reveal a secret miniature world. Ivy, honeysuckle and wild rose ramble over crumbling walls, their leaves and branches providing cover and food for birds and insect life. In autumn, berries ripen amongst golden leaves.

Fig. 12.1
Casket designed by Nicola Jarvis and stitched by
Karen Goldie-Morrison. © Photo David Gowers.

Fig. 12.2
Working on the
front panel.
© Photo Lynn
Hulse.

Fig. 12.3
Front and back
panels before
mounting.
© Photo David
Gowers.

13 Deborah Jarman

I created this box over four years with the support of workshops held at the Ashmolean Museum in Oxford. The Museum has a large collection of raised work, a type of embroidery that was very fashionable in the mid to late seventeenth century. It was often used to decorate boxes and mirror frames.

The design on the top of my box was adapted from a panel made in 1673. The front and back panels are a celebration of my home in Herefordshire. On one side, you can see a picture of my house (a converted hop barn with two oast houses) with our two Dalmatian dogs, and on the other side, a view of our garden and the fields of the Frome valley beyond, complete with pond and a Herefordshire bullock, which has pushed his way through the hedge! We can just see the Malvern Hills from our front gate. On one short end, you can see the Malverns at night, and on the other, the colours of a winter sunrise over the hills.

All the plants on the frieze and side panels grow in our garden – hops, wisteria, jasmine, apple blossom and raspberries.

Fig. 13.1
Casket designed by Nicola Jarvis and stitched by Deborah Jarman. © Photo David Gowers.

Fig. 13.2
Working on the
front panel.
© Photo Lynn
Hulse.

Fig. 13.3
Front and back
panels before
mounting.
© Photo Lynn
Hulse.

14 Clare Lobb

My garden and feline family have been very much part of my life so I have chosen to display three panels: the garden seat, a place where I can sit and relax with a cup of coffee in the morning sun accompanied by my cat, Frodo; the garden shed which houses various gardening paraphernalia and a favourite place of Finzi; and, the kitten frieze. As each sibling has a unique character, I have depicted Frodo, looking as he always did, slightly grumpy, and Finzi's gentle demeanour and quiet contentment.

The garden also has wonderful memories of my dear, late husband, Donald, who would enjoy this special place, and like me, absorb the beauty and quietness of our small garden filled with sweet smelling blooms, as depicted in the urn and pots.

Unfortunately both my cats now reside in a different garden but their spirits will always be in our earthly garden.

Fig. 14.1
Casket panel designed by Nicola Jarvis and stitched by Clare Lobb. © Photo David Gowers.

Fig. 14.2
Casket panel
designed by
Nicola Jarvis
and stitched by
Clare Lobb.
© Photo Lynn
Hulse.

Fig. 14.3
Work in
progress on the
frieze panels
designed by
Nicola Jarvis
and stitched by
Clare Lobb.
© Photo David
Gowers.

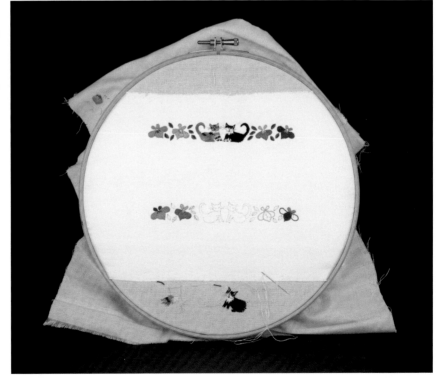

15 Jane McConnachie

This box lid is worked in Soie d'Alger on canvas. The inspiration came from trying to recreate this Northamptonshire seventeenth-century cottage called 'Owls Hoot' (a three-dimensional barn owl can be seen perching in the tree) and the charming St Peters Church in Cogenhoe. The main stitches used are tent, upright cross and straight and encroaching gobelin, with bullion knots for the wisteria. There are so many colours in the sandstone and ironstone that it was a joy to blend them in my needle in order to try and give a true representation of the beautiful Northamptonshire stone. Whilst working on this project I was reminded of embroiderers in past centuries and the challenges they faced with poor light and not so many colours to use in order to complete their work.

Fig. 15.1
Casket designed by Nicola Jarvis and stitched by Jane McConnachie. © Photo David Gowers.

Fig. 15.2
Casket lid. © Photo Jane McConnachie.

16 Suzanne Morton

The Norfolk Box

This casket depicts the River Yare at Norwich, Horsey Staithe, the cliffs at Hunstanton and my home. The border of the lid features sweet peas and butterflies, including a purple edged copper, a Camberwell beauty, an Adonis blue and a tortoiseshell.

The flowers surrounding my home are snowdrops, snowflakes, primroses, daffodils, cyclamen, violets, crocuses and snakes head fritillaries. A red admiral butterfly flutters above.

Around the cliffs at Hunstanton are sea-lavender, red and white clover, buttercup, daisies, cowslips, heather, bush vetch white cinquefoil, sea sandwort and round headed leek.

The River Yare has common scabious, lady's smock, violas, Christmas roses and forget-me-nots, with an Adonis blue butterfly.

Horsey Staithe has bulrushes, Lords-and-Ladies, flag iris, lavender, waterlilies and rushes with a dragonfly and an orange-tip butterfly.

Inside the base of the box are silk shaded waterlilies.

Fig. 16.1
Casket designed by Nicola Jarvis and stitched by Suzanne Morton. © Photo David Gowers.

Fig. 16.2
Frieze and back
panel, 'Horsey
Staithe'.
© Photo
Lynn Hulse.

Fig. 16.3
Frieze and side
panel with an
image of
Suzanne's
home.
© Photo Lynn
Hulse.

17 Jenny Plumb

I am the eldest of four girls and grew up in a home where we all sewed and knitted and made our own clothes. The one craft I never mastered was embroidery. Most fortuitously I joined classes held by *Ornamental Embroidery* at the Ashmolean where I was gently encouraged by Lynn Hulse and Nicola Jarvis to attempt the raised work casket. Almost five years and many hours of stitching later you see the finished article in front of you.

I was born in South Africa of a Scottish mother and Dutch father. I spent the first third of my life there. My box reflects in stitch the important images in my life. The frieze represent the seasons and flowers that are special to me such as the Scottish thistle, the bluebells that grow in our garden, the primroses that pop up in the lawn every spring and the sunflowers that filled the farms in Kroonstad.

I trained as a cardiac theatre nurse in Cape Town at Groote Schuur Hospital (Groote Schuur means big barn in Afrikaans) The front of the box depicts a Cape Dutch house with a silhouette of Table Mountain in the background. Agapanthus and Protea are found in abundance in Kirstenbosch gardens, which nestle against Table Mountain. The hummingbird is commonly found gathering nectar from the local Cape Flora.

Fig. 17.1
Casket designed by Nicola Jarvis and stitched by Jenny Plumb. © Photo David Gowers.

I moved to England when I married an Englishman, whose family farmed cherries in Oxfordshire. My husband's parents lived in a sixteenth-century thatched cottage bordered by an avenue of walnuts planted by an ancestor. There were always hollyhocks in front of the property and a single, yellow peony known as 'Molly the Witch'.

The smaller sides remind me of flock of geese I kept in my garden for many years before a crafty fox eventually left us without any. The animals we had while my children were growing were Old English Sheep dogs and we have always had Siamese cats. The animals on the side panel are in recognition of them.

Fig. 17.2
Back panel with Oxfordshire thatched cottage. © Photo Lynn Hulse.

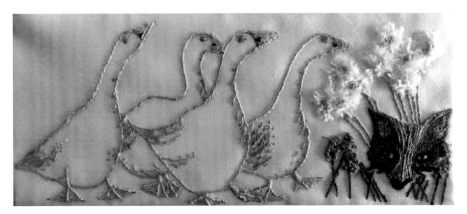

Fig. 17.3
Side panel with geese and fox. © Photo Lynn Hulse.

18 Ann Stainton

Family Tree

I have always loved raised work and felt inspired by seventeenth-century caskets. Having completed the *Oak Tree* panel, my box evolved into an heirloom project. The long sides represent my parents and my children, depicted through heritage and interests, and the short sides show the next generation as trees bearing fruit.

My Irish mother, a great knitter, is the ball of green wool surrounded by a Celtic knot with knitting needles behind. The fuschias bring back holidays in Ireland where they grow wild in the hedgerows. My daughter, a voracious reader who loved fossils, became a geologist, hence the book and ammonite.

My father is the Hampshire rose with oars behind. My elder son studied chemistry and went into banking (the bubbling flask and £ sign). My younger son trampolined for Great Britain and teaches music (the trampoline and guitar).

The ring of individual wild strawberries on the frieze reminds me of picking them in my grandparents' garden. Their roots spread into all our own gardens.

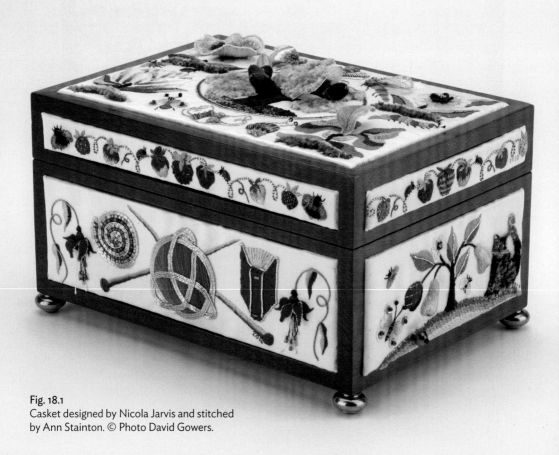

Fig. 18.1
Casket designed by Nicola Jarvis and stitched
by Ann Stainton. © Photo David Gowers.

As family life has changed, the elements of my casket have gained relevance. We have extended the Celtic knot to include Welsh and Irish in-laws and enriched the link with butterflies. My father's oars have pride of place in the garden by the river and the ladybird could be me, the one who hid under the frying pan!

Huge thanks to Nicola Jarvis and Lynn Hulse for the inspiration behind the project. Nicola's design skills took the ideas from my head to fabric and Lynn's knowledge supported my interpretations. Their enthusiasm and encouragement kept the project alive.

Fig. 18.2
Front and back panels before mounting.
© Photo David Gowers.

Fig. 18.3
Frieze panels before mounting.
© Photo David Gowers.

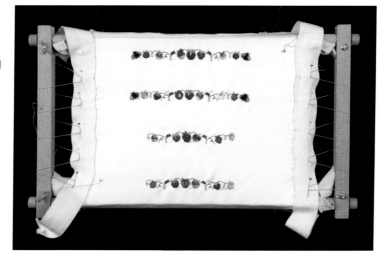

Contributors

Dr Mary Brooks trained as a textile conservator at the Textile Conservation Centre and the Abegg Stiftung, Switzerland, and subsequently worked at the De Young Museum, San Francisco and York Castle Museum. She became Head of Studies and Research at the Textile Conservation Centre and is now at Durham University. Her research interests include seventeenth-century embroideries, the use of X-radiography for the greater understanding of textiles and dress, ecclesiastical vestments and regenerated protein fibres.

Jacqui Carey has been a practising craftsperson since completing her BA (Hons) degree in Textiles in 1985. In 2005, Jacqui became a QEST scholar for her work in analysing historic structures and techniques, and was awarded an MA (distinction) in the History of Textile & Dress from the Textile Conservation Centre. Jacqui's willingness to share her expertise has seen her exhibit and teach worldwide. She is also the author of over ten books, including *Elizabethan Stitches: A Guide to Historic English Needlework* (2012).

Dr Lynn Hulse has focused on embroidered textiles since 2004. She worked as Archivist at the Royal School of Needlework (2004-2010) and was a Visiting Research Fellow at the Victoria and Albert Museum (2015-2017). Lynn is a Fellow of the Society of Antiquaries of London, Chair of the Trustees of the Brangwyn Gift at the William Morris Gallery and Co-founder of *Ornamental Embroidery*. Her research interests include the development of art embroidery during the second half of the nineteenth century.

Nicola Jarvis trained at the Royal School of Needlework and worked on the lace for the Duchess of Cambridge's wedding dress in 2011. Her debut solo exhibition, *The Art of Embroidery: Nicola Jarvis and May Morris*, was staged at the William Morris Gallery in 2013. Supported by Arts Council England, she toured this popular display around selected Arts and Crafts venues in the UK until 2016. Nicola teaches internationally and received a Commendation from the Beryl Dean Award for Teaching Excellence in 2018. Her embroidery design business *Nicola Jarvis Studio* supplies many clients, including John Lewis and the National Trust.

Susan Stanton has been Textile Conservator at the Ashmolean Museum since 1996, and has worked on the conservation, display and storage of the English embroidery pieces in the Museum's collection. She trained at the Textile Conservation Centre, Hampton Court and has also worked for the Area Museum Council for the South West.